OAE

Assessment of Professional Knowledge: Middle Childhood (4-9) Practice Questions

Mometrix

TEST PREPARATION

Dear Future Exam Success Story

First of all, **THANK YOU** for purchasing Mometrix study materials!

Second, congratulations! You are one of the few determined test-takers who are committed to doing whatever it takes to excel on your exam. **You have come to the right place.** We developed these practice tests with one goal in mind: to deliver you the best possible approximation of the questions you will see on test day.

Standardized testing is one of the biggest obstacles on your road to success, which only increases the importance of doing well in the high-pressure, high-stakes environment of test day. Your results on this test could have a significant impact on your future, and these practice tests will give you the repetitions you need to build your familiarity and confidence with the test content and format to help you achieve your full potential on test day.

Your success is our success

We would love to hear from you! If you would like to share the story of your exam success or if you have any questions or comments in regard to our products, please contact us at **800-673-8175** or **support@mometrix.com**.

Thanks again for your business and we wish you continued success!

Sincerely,
The Mometrix Test Preparation Team

TABLE OF CONTENTS

Practice Test #1

1. Which of the following is one way teachers can help adolescent students develop their pragmatic linguistic skills?

a. Teach them to distinguish literal vs. figurative word meanings.
b. Teach them the skills needed to ask others questions socially.
c. Increase their vocabularies to increase their intellectual ability.
d. There is no specific instruction for developing pragmatic skills.

2. When sixth-graders fail to complete assignments or act out in class, to which of the following are teachers with experience and developmental perspectives more likely to attribute such events accurately, whereas teachers without these assets are more likely to choose one of the others?

a. ADHD
b. Mental illnesses
c. Behavioral problems
d. Adjustment problems

3. Which of the following can teachers incorporate in instruction with adolescent students that they could not with younger students?

a. Liquid conservation
b. Deductive reasoning
c. Reversible operations
d. Symbolic representation

4. Of the following, which is the MOST accurate conclusion regarding cultural differences in American middle schools and high schools, particularly about school desegregation and bilingual education?

a. Since American schools today are desegregated, the neighborhoods surrounding them must also be.
b. Since some Latino parents feel it can overcome discrimination, bilingual education must be required.
c. Since school desegregation and appropriate services for English leaners are both legal mandates, compromise is needed.
d. Since some Latino parents think it ruins Latin influence and bilingual programs, desegregation is bad.

5. Which of these most describes developmental activities of *later* adolescence?

a. Establishing realistic goals for life and pursuing them
b. Applying cognitive skills and developing self-images
c. Separating from parents, exploring, experimenting
d. Developing responsibility, self-reliance, and control

6. Hands-on, experiential learning activities can further adolescent cognitive and psychosocial development. Which result of these activities is most likely to help preadolescents and younger adolescents resolve the conflict of Industry vs. Inferiority?

a. Transitioning from concrete to abstract thought
b. Having experiences of success in school activity
c. Forming future action plans they find satisfying
d. Transitioning from intuitive to logical reasoning

7. Which of the following is the most appropriate example of an assignment that a teacher can give to students in grades 10-12?

a. Setting positive social interaction goals; distinguishing between short-term goals and long-term goals
b. Setting long-term goals with action steps, completion dates, anticipated obstacles, contingency plans
c. Setting short-term goals, planning action steps and time frames, evaluating levels of goal achievement
d. Setting long-term goals; analyzing impacts of obstacles, conflicts, opportunities on goal achievement

8. Which kinds of instructional approaches best address the developmental characteristics and needs of adolescents?

a. Providing hands-on, real-world, and authentic learning experiences
b. Providing narrower ranges of learning materials for focus and depth
c. Providing simpler, more concrete information, concepts, and humor
d. Providing traditional academic content to ensure strong foundations

9. Researcher Robert Pianta (c. 2012) compared two approaches to changing teacher expectations. One approach was to talk to teachers, giving them information to persuade them that they held erroneous beliefs. The other approach was to give teachers intensive training in practicing different classroom behaviors. What were the results?

a. Teachers' beliefs were changed more by the behavioral training.
b. Teachers' beliefs were changed more by the informational talks.
c. Teachers' beliefs were changed equally by both the approaches.
d. Teachers' beliefs were not changed by either of the approaches.

10. Which of the following is a common expert recommendation that allows teachers to address problematic student behaviors?

a. Teachers cannot and should not try to view school through students' eyes.
b. Teachers' own experiences with teachers, either good or bad, are irrelevant.
c. Teachers should list words that describe their feelings when interacting with teachers/supervisors and what evoked them.
d. Teachers should focus on their perceptions of students but not vice versa.

11. What is true about an effective instructional strategy that improves teaching effectiveness and student performance

a. Teachers' telling students success stories will not help them see cause and effect.
b. Teachers should have students keep logs to help them connect efforts to results.
c. Teachers' tangible rewards to students are more effective than symbolic rewards.
d. Teachers should ensure equitable treatment by making student rewards uniform.

12. What is correct regarding teacher use of words and images in instruction?

a. Visual representations are preferred since they stimulate and increase brain activity.
b. Verbal representations are preferred for instructing students regarding relationships.
c. Visuals are better for relationships; verbal modes are better for teaching information.
d. Students achieve more when they are taught using both verbal and visual modalities.

13. Which of these statements accurately reflects recommended practices for giving students learning goals and feedback?

a. Learning goals for students should be unrelated to their personal goals.
b. Contracts are good ways to define goals and grades for reaching them.
c. Teachers should give students general, delayed, and positive feedback.
d. Teachers should be the only ones who lead student feedback sessions.

14. Schools can engage students in activities enabling their participation in school-based issues to promote critical thinking and ownership of learning. Which example correctly matches the student role with the associated activity?

a. Students as planners in classroom behavior rules, new building design, choosing textbooks
b. Students as professional development partners in showing teachers how to use technology
c. Students as decision makers in collecting and analyzing data and team development activity
d. Students as teachers in influencing curriculum, school policy, and school climate in governing

15. What correctly reflects a principle about helping middle and high school students with summarizing content, taking notes, studying, and using advance organizers?

a. Given time, students can often study best for tests by reviewing and revising their notes.
b. Skimming text, storytelling, and graphic images are unrelated to using advance organizers.
c. Advance organizers should be holistic and introduced after lessons but in advance of tests.
d. Questioning, clarifying, and predicting text helps students understand but not summarize.

16. Which of the following is true about teaching secondary school students how to conduct research for writing research papers?

a. In identifying sources, teaching students MLA, APA, or Turabian style will enable plagiarism.
b. In identifying sources, teaching students fair use and copyright laws can prevent plagiarism.
c. In identifying sources, teaching students about Creative Commons will guarantee plagiarism.
d. In identifying sources, teaching students to evaluate them is the sole way to stop plagiarism.

17. Which choice correctly sequences these related behavior disorders by age groups affected, from youngest to oldest?

a. Antisocial Personality Disorder, Oppositional Defiant Disorder, Conduct Disorder
b. Conduct Disorder, Antisocial Personality Disorder, Oppositional Defiant Disorder
c. Oppositional Defiant Disorder, Conduct Disorder, Antisocial Personality Disorder
d. These behavior disorders are not related and do not affect particular age groups

18. Of the following adaptations, which most helps visually impaired students navigate school buildings and grounds and other public environments?

a. Strobe lights
b. Text-to-speech software
c. Magnification and large print
d. Orientation and mobility training

19. Tantrums, "meltdowns," interruptions, and other disruptive and/or inappropriate classroom behaviors are most common with which type(s) of behavior disorder(s)?

a. Intellectual disabilities
b. With any or all of these
c. Autism spectrum disorders
d. Attention deficit hyperactivity disorder

20. Which of the following is an example of how the variable of gender can affect student learning and performance?

a. Visual vs. kinesthetic
b. Cooperation vs. competition
c. Physical vs. relational aggression
d. Inadequate vs. adequate clothes/food

21. Whether a student has more internal or external locus of control is related to which variable influencing learning and achievement?

a. Motivation
b. Self-confidence
c. Student maturity
d. Cognitive development

22. What law(s) were models on which the Americans with Disabilities Act (ADA) was modeled?

a. The Civil Rights Act
b. The Rehabilitation Act
c. The Individuals with Disabilities Education Act
d. (a) and (b) were, but (c) under that name was not

23. Which of the following accurately reflects a provision of the IDEA?

a. Separate classes/schools for students with disabilities
b. Meeting student needs that differ among individuals
c. Requiring IEPs for all students with/without disabilities
d. Enacted at the same time for school and younger ages

24. Among the following laws, which specifically require schools receiving federal funds to provide students with eligible disabilities a "free, appropriate public education (FAPE)"?

a. The ADA and Section 504
b. The ADA and the IDEA do
c. Section 504 and the IDEA
d. All three of these laws do

25. Which of the following defines discriminant validity in assessment?

a. Constructs are not combined or confounded in what a test measures.
b. Constructs expected to be related when tested are found to be related.
c. Constructs expected to be unrelated are tested and are found unrelated.
d. Constructs measured by tests can be generalized to the larger population.

26. An educational researcher gives the same test to two groups of students, then delivers an instructional intervention to one group, and then gives both groups the same test again. The intervention/treatment group scores much higher this time; the control (non-treatment) group scores essentially the same as the first time. The researcher concludes that barring other factors, the intervention was what raised one group's scores. What type of validity does this illustrate?

a. Internal validity
b. External validity
c. Ecological validity
d. Population validity

27. Which statement is most accurate in describing formal assessments?

a. They are best for formative assessment.
b. They are frequently standardized tests.
c. They are more individualized measures.
d. They are typically criterion referenced.

28. Of the following, which most correctly represents informal assessments?

a. These are supported with statistics.
b. These are best for generalized data.
c. These are best to compare students.
d. These are often performance based.

29. What is more typical of an informal assessment?

a. Assessing overall achievement
b. Improving ongoing instruction
c. Yielding more objective results
d. Being scored with percentiles

30. When teachers assess student performance using continua, which of the following is considered a disadvantage?

a. More precise evaluative descriptions of student performance instead of discrete grades
b. Greater difficulty in comparing student, class, and school scores without exact numbers
c. Performance ranges are more realistic and accurate than exact numbers or cutoff scores
d. Greater compatibility with individualized student assessment than standardized testing

31. Which of these do standardized ability tests measure in students?

a. Student competence
b. Student performance
c. Student school grades
d. Student mental health

32. What is correct in describing standardized achievement tests?

a. They measure convergent and divergent thinking and domain-specific skills.
b. They measure what students are capable of as well as what they actually do.
c. They are formative evaluations, frequently made during ongoing instruction.
d. They are summative evaluations, usually given at the end of the school year.

33. What do standardized achievement test results enable educators to do?

a. They enable educators to compare students in one grade to those in other grades.
b. They enable educators to assess student fulfillment of classroom learning criteria.
c. They enable educators to compare an individual student's progress over the years.
d. They enable educators to compare achievement among students but not schools.

34. Which of these do standardized ability tests and standardized aptitude tests both do?

a. Both measure execution, not potential.
b. Both measure potential, not execution.
c. Both measure potential plus execution.
d. Both measure ability and also interests.

35. Which of the following best reflects theoretical bases for standards-based education?

a. Reporting annual standardized test results
b. Giving low grades for poor initial performance
c. Norm-referenced summative assessment scores
d. Frequent formative criterion-referenced feedback

36. What is true regarding funding for, development of, and access to federal and state curriculum standards?

a. The US Department of Education funds and develops standards.
b. Standards and updates are now easier to access online than in print.
c. State education departments fund and develop these standards.
d. Adopting the Common Core State Standards is a federal mandate.

37. Which of these is a benefit of federal and state curriculum standards and frameworks?

a. Giving stakeholders common educational partnership language
b. Making individual school and district systems function uniquely
c. Varying expectations for students according to individual needs
d. Freeing schools to focus, design, and plan their own instruction

38. When analyzing examples of student learning in Physical Education, which of the following activities are representative of the affective domain?

a. The student reads some text about physical exercise; understands it, analyzes it, and compares it to other information sources.
b. The student observes, imitates, practices, and perfects the specific physical skills required to engage in a specific sport s/he prefers.
c. The student shows s/he values exercise knowledge by voluntary athletic participation and becomes accomplished in a specific sport.
d. The student judges some information about physical exercise according to established criteria and writes a paper about the topic.

39. Which of the following correctly reflects the hierarchy of Bloom's Taxonomy in its most recent (2001) revision?

a. Understanding information comes before remembering it.
b. The analysis of information comes before its application.
c. The organization is by types, not by levels of difficulty.
d. Evaluation of information comes before its creation.

40. How are instructional objectives that apply Bloom's Taxonomy also influenced by a major principle of behaviorist learning theory?

a. They use Bloom's Taxonomy terms requiring students to remember and understand.
b. They use only action verbs to describe how students must demonstrate their learning.
c. They use only behaviorist methods of changing behavior for teaching new information.
d. They use only behaviors that can be externally observed, whether measurable or not.

41. In the learning objective, "Writing at a fifth-grade reading level, given a sentence in past tense, the student will rewrite it to future tense correctly 95 percent of the time," which part represents the "D" element of the ABCD method for writing observable, measurable learning objectives?

a. At fifth-grade reading level
b. Correctly 95 percent of the time
c. Rewrite it to future tense
d. A sentence in past tense

42. Which of these is the most important element among criteria for evaluating technological and other instructional resources in schools and districts?

a. Criteria for evaluating individual instructional technology items
b. Criteria for evaluating instructional materials less authentically
c. Criteria for evaluating the practicability of any instructional unit
d. Criteria for evaluating based on national, not district standards

43. Of the following, which represents a teacher professional learning resource rather than a student learning material?

a. Research articles
b. Manipulatives
c. Worksheets
d. Games

44. What is a purpose and characteristic of thematic instruction?

a. Teaching cognitive skills in the context of academic subjects
b. Teaching broadly enough to enable creative exploration
c. Teaching specifically enough for practical applications
d. Teaching both (b) and (c) rather than only (a)

45. Which of the following is an example of experiential learning?

a. Watching a video, taking notes
b. Reading a textbook, taking notes
c. Testing a hypothesis, taking notes
d. Listening to a lecture, taking notes

46. Interactive learning activities can overlap with which other instructional methods?

a. Indirect instruction activities
b. Independent study activities
c. Experiential learning activities
d. With any, for certain activities

47. When should teachers write lesson plans for effective organization and implementation?

a. After creating the plan of study but before the lesson plan calendar
b. After a plan of study, units, timelines, and lesson plan calendar
c. After planning instructional unit but before planning timelines
d. After making a lesson plan calendar but before planning the units

48. Which of these is a benefit students receive from continuous student performance monitoring and charting?

a. Students receive visual illustrations of what they learn.
b. Students receive delayed feedback from the teachers.
c. Students receive graphs and goals only from a teacher.
d. Students receive practice through independent study.

49. Which statement is most accurate about the instructional approach of using scaffolding?

a. It ultimately moves student roles in learning from active to passive.
b. It ultimately requires students to maintain their current knowledge.
c. It ultimately moves learning responsibility from teacher to student.
d. It ultimately moves teacher roles from facilitator/mentor to expert.

50. In scaffolded instruction, what is the correct sequence (first to last) of these steps?

a. Teacher modeling, student think-alouds; student-teacher collaboration; student paired/small-group work, scaffolded as needed; independent student practice
b. Independent student practice; student-teacher collaboration; teacher modeling, student think-alouds; student paired/small-group work, scaffolded as needed
c. Student-teacher collaboration; student paired/small-group work, scaffolded as needed; independent student practice; teacher modeling, student think-alouds
d. Student paired/small-group work, scaffolded as needed; teacher modeling, student think-alouds; independent student practice; student-teacher collaboration

51. Which of these represents a caveat concerning independent instruction?

a. Students can pursue individual interests with their own paces and styles.
b. Students develop autonomy, initiative, self-confidence, and self-esteem.
c. Students benefit from the high flexibility and adaptability of applications.
d. Students must first have developed skills needed to work independently.

Refer to the following for question 52:

Mrs. Jacobs teaches a careers class. She wants her students to be more engaged in their learning, so she decides to break them into groups and have each team research and present a lesson on a career of the group's choosing. Each member of the team is assigned a task and will be graded on their individual and group efforts. One group decides to focus on a career in the environmental field. Matt is a student in this group, and after doing the initial research, he seems very interested in considering it as a future career. He wants to study this topic in greater depth, develop specific expertise in sustainable practices, and research other environmental jobs to consider as future career paths.

52. Which type of classroom learning center would best help Matt accomplish all of his goals?

a. Any or all of these
b. An enrichment center
c. A skill development center
d. An interest/exploratory center

53. In independent instruction, what is included in student research projects?

a. Teachers assign research questions for students to investigate.
b. Students develop research questions; teachers supply sources.
c. Teachers provide guidance to students only as needed.
d. Students must communicate their results without any guidance.

Refer to the following for question 54:

Mrs. Schubert is taking her biology class on a field trip to the local natural science museum. They have just finished a unit on world biomes, and the museum has exhibits on desert flora and fauna as well as wetland life.

54. What is most true about how field trips like this relate to student learning?

a. Their only benefit is that students love getting out of the classroom.
b. They have the benefits of applying classroom knowledge in real life.
c. They confuse students when real conditions differ from classrooms.
d. They give the benefit of interacting with nature but offer no real learning.

55. Of the following learning activities, which kind are *not* done in real life but are the *most realistic* of those not done in real life?

a. Field trips
b. Simulations
c. Experiments
d. Role-playing

56. Which statement is most correct about the following instructional strategies?

a. Simulations using technology are no different than those without it.
b. As instructional activities, games are entertaining but lack structure.
c. Observations develop objectivity, detail orientation, and perception.
d. Experiments have no effect on abstract concepts or student attitude.

57. Which of the following is true of intrinsic student motivation?

a. It tends to last longer than external motivation.
b. It tends to take less time to foster than external motivation.
c. It is generally less effective at motivating success than external motivation.
d. Few students can be intrinsically motivated in school

58. What is true about how teachers can support student development of intrinsic motivation?

a. Teachers can interest students in content without being interested in it themselves.
b. Teachers strongly interested in content need not show it to develop this motivation.
c. Teachers can develop intrinsic student motivation without knowing student interests.
d. Teachers can develop intrinsic motivation by connecting content to student interests.

59. Research-based strategies to motivate students are reflected by which teacher behavior?

a. They are interested in students' learning but are not personally interested.
b. They are role models, leading student motivation and passion by example.
c. They need not believe in students' abilities as long as they indicate interest.
d. They eschew the personalization of subject content for individual students.

60. Among research-based strategies to enhance student motivation, what is applicable?

a. Students will be overwhelmed by being given too many examples.
b. Students must be taught underlying principles directly by teachers.
c. Students often want to know how content is relevant to their lives.
d. Students succeed in cooperative learning groups without pressure.

61. What can teachers do in terms of assignments, goals, and assessment to motivate student learning?

a. Design assignments that give every student the same challenge.
b. Set, and help students set, performance goals that are realistic.
c. Use tests scores and grades to indicate students' shortcomings.
d. Grade tests on a curve to enable all students to get high grades.

62. To communicate effectively with all students in diverse classrooms, which of these is NOT a recommended teacher technique for transitions between topics?

a. Implicit transitions requiring student inferences
b. Verbal signals to the students about transitions
c. Making mini-summaries of the preceding topics
d. Establishing some connections between topics

63. Which of the following accurately reflects effective teacher verbal communication strategies with all students?

a. Teachers should keep vocal speeds and tones uniform to enhance student comprehension.
b. Teachers who project their voices only intimidate students and do not help hearing.
c. Teachers get attention, show transitions, and enable processing via strategic pauses.
d. Teachers should accord the same wait times for ELL and disabled students as others.

64. Which of these is true about effective nonverbal communication by teachers?

a. Unusual or flashy apparel and exaggerated gestures are effective.
b. Appropriate movements expressing energy and enthusiasm work.
c. Students will not take teachers who smile while teaching seriously.
d. Relaxed posture and avoiding eye contact will put students at ease.

65. In teacher communication strategies, what best describes the effects of some types?

a. Utilizing media will only distract from communicating instructionally.
b. Slide presentations demonstrate reasoning and illustrate processes.
c. Animations and videos are best for the summarization of key points.
d. Boards or overheads show reasoning visually and illustrate processes.

66. Among the following instructional aids, which is best for illustrating sounds associated with physical processes?

a. Audio
b. Realia
c. Artifacts
d. Handouts

67. Based on research findings, how does role-playing contribute to effective conflict resolution in the classroom?

a. Role-playing makes conflicts appear less humorous.
b. Role-playing focuses students on their own feelings.
c. Role-playing teaches perspective-taking and empathy.
d. Role-playing promotes subjective reactions to conflict.

68. Which of these most accurately reflects expert recommendations of effective strategies for resolving classroom conflicts?

a. De-emphasize conflicts by not letting students record them.
b. Have students record observations, identifying participants.
c. Discuss student reactions without judging them good or bad.
d. Have students track conflicts over time and discuss reactions.

69. Informed by research results, experts on conflict resolution recommend which of the following as good listening behaviors for teachers to impart to students?

a. Asking questions as needed, but not interrupting others
b. Avoiding embarrassing others by not making eye contact
c. Giving others suggestions or advice about what they said
d. Staying objective by not nodding/smiling as others speak

70. When students have been involved in classroom conflicts, what does it accomplish for teachers to have them write about these?

a. It makes them ruminate about and extend conflicts.
b. It gives them time out for cooling off and reflecting.
c. It helps them review their feelings, not alternatives.
d. It keeps them from learning anything from conflicts.

71. As an approach for managing student behavior, what is a characteristic of the "simple authority statement" from the teacher?

a. It causes emotional distress but stops misbehavior authoritatively.
b. It models reasonable, respectful use of authority with little upset.
c. It expresses teacher disapproval of student behavior subjectively.
d. It expresses teacher disapproval authoritatively, but it takes time.

72. What is true about teachers' treating students the same way regardless of how much or little they expect from them?

a. Doing this is easier affectively than academically.
b. Doing this is difficult affectively and academically.
c. Doing this is easy affectively and/or academically.
d. Doing this is easier academically than affectively.

73. Which of these is accurate regarding teacher strategies for responding to student cultural diversity needs?

a. To make diversity a resource, not a liability, do not give students adult responsibilities.
b. To fill gaps in cultural capital, explicitly teach skills for studying and college preparation.
c. To foster student participation, avoid showing personal interest in individual students.
d. To understand student behavior in and out of class, knowing home cultures is no help.

74. Which of the following is correct regarding parents and education?

a. The way parents converse has no effect on their children's classroom communications.
b. Educators need not be as concerned about parent expectations as school expectations.
c. Educators can help parents pursue ESL and GED programs, which support their children.
d. Referring students' parents to community resources is outside the scope for educators.

75. Which statement is most accurate about culturally relevant instruction?

a. Making semantic webs about student experiences cannot inform lesson planning.
b. Culturally relevant curriculum aids authentic, interactive literacy and thinking skills.
c. Students' self-esteem is unaffected by curriculum on their cultures' contributions.
d. Culturally compatible norms make topics meaningful but do not affect instruction.

76. Among instructional techniques to develop oral communication skills, which one would incorporate "CROWD" and "PEER" prompts?

a. Dialogic Reading
b. Think-Pair-Share
c. Choral Response
d. Inside/Outside Circle

77. Which teaching strategy for developing written communication skills can also be used to develop spoken communication skills?

a. Written Responses, Varying Answers
b. Written Responses, Same Answers
c. None of these work for both
d. Think-Pair-Share activities

78. What is most accurate about traditional vs. cooperative organized games for preschoolers?

a. Other than their organization, these have essentially the same effects.
b. Cooperative games are less fun for children than traditional games are.
c. Traditional games are better than cooperative for teaching varied skills.
d. Preschoolers have more fun and learn more skills in cooperative games.

79. For kindergarteners, what must teachers consider in scheduling learning activities?

a. High energy levels mean children need ongoing active movement.
b. Extended activities are best for developing longer attention spans.
c. Alternating movement and rest prevents exhaustion and boredom.
d. Kindergarteners cannot work independently or cooperatively yet.

80. For younger students, which skills does play develop?

a. Social skills but not academic skills
b. Social and all main academic skills
c. Literacy and math, but not others
d. Most subjects but not technology

81. According to teachers and administrators, which is accurate about strategies for parent-teacher conferences they recommend?

a. Parents usually resent ideas for home use from teachers.
b. Thanking parents for attending conferences is important.
c. Parents will not want specific suggestions on how to help.
d. Needed improvements discussed require no follow-ups.

82. Regarding parent-teacher conferences, what reflects teacher reports of effective strategies?

a. Blunt phrasing is the only way to get students and parents to see reality.
b. Teachers should never include students in conferences with the parents.
c. Some teachers let students lead conferences on report cards, portfolios.
d. Teachers should avoid setting goals with students and parents too early.

83. What is true about teacher participation in school/district committees and activities?

a. Teachers may only serve on committees during school days.
b. Committee work enables problem solving for teachers only.
c. Teachers communicate with parents, not involving students.
d. Teacher support often determines extracurricular activities.

84. Which of the following is true about participation in committees, projects, and other school functions?

a. Participation provides more chances to pursue professional development.
b. Participation in these is generally not worth the time due to a lack of relation to in-class work.
c. These functions focus on information that spans across a wide range of domains instead of focusing on individual content subjects.
d. Participation in sporting events is generally required.

85. Which of the following is true regarding how teachers can participate in school or district projects, committees, and other activities?

a. Teachers can only participate in faculty, department, staff, and PTA/PTO meetings.
b. Teachers' participation is only beneficial to students and other teachers.
c. Teachers are unqualified to join committees concerned with the admission of special populations.
d. Teachers can find and choose texts for educational use and contribute to curriculum design.

86. Experts report which of the following about reflective teachers relative to appraisals?

a. Reflective teachers excel at self-evaluation but resist others' evaluations.
b. Reflective teachers do not fear evaluations but are unlikely to self-assess.
c. Reflective teachers want self-improvement informed by other educators.
d. Reflective teachers are motivated to improve mainly for better appraisals.

87. Which of the following is true about who usually conducts teacher appraisals?

a. School administrators, like the principal, generally conduct appraisals.
b. Third-party evaluators are used to ensure no bias in appraisals.
c. Colleagues, such as fellow teachers, usually conduct appraisals because they have expertise in teaching.
d. District-level officials usually conduct appraisals for the schools in their jurisdiction.

88. Among areas wherein appraisal systems evaluate teacher performance, what is or is not included?

a. Effective instruction, teacher-centered or student-centered regardless
b. Whether students participate actively and successfully in their learning
c. Evaluation of student progress is more important than giving feedback
d. Discipline is not evaluated like time, materials, and teaching strategies

89. What is correct about how teachers are evaluated in performance appraisal systems?

a. Professional communication is not an appraised topic.
b. Professional development for the teacher is included.
c. Compliance with policies and procedures for operations is not evaluated.
d. Only improvement for identified students is assessed.

90. Which of the following is true about teacher appraisals?

a. They are conducted based on federal guidelines.
b. They are used primarily to ensure teacher attendance.
c. They are usually conducted by third-party evaluators.
d. They are generally regulated at the local level.

91. FERPA regulations allow student records disclosure without consent under which conditions?

a. To any school officials, who need not have specific reasons
b. To schools where students transfer so records are needed
c. To school personnel excepting those related to financial aid
d. To any auditing or evaluating officials with no specifications

92. Which of the following is FALSE according to the provisions of FERPA?

a. Schools may furnish student records without consent to researchers performing studies on behalf of the school.
b. Schools may furnish student records without consent when issued court orders and subpoenas.
c. Schools may furnish student records without consent in the event of a safety or health emergency.
d. Schools may furnish student records without consent to juvenile justice system authorities in all states.

93. What is correct about FERPA regulations regarding school disclosure of student directory information?

a. Schools must obtain written consent from the student's parents prior to disclosure.
b. Schools can disclose names, addresses, and birth dates, but not phone numbers.
c. Schools must notify parents and students of FERPA rights but must not disclose.
d. Schools can only disclose with enough prior notice for requesting non-disclosure.

94. Which of the following professional organizations is a labor union?

a. National Education Association
b. National Association for the Education of Young Children
c. Association for Supervision and Curriculum Development
d. National Council of Teachers of English

95. What is true about the professional organizations available to educators today?

a. Early childhood education has its own professional organization.
b. Organizations exist for science teachers but not specific sciences.
c. There is a special education group, but none for gifted education.
d. An organization exists for teaching foreign languages but not ESL.

96. Which professional development resource most often informs teachers about the effectiveness of various instructional practices?

a. Federal education departments
b. Educational research studies
c. State boards of education
d. Local school districts

97. What is applicable regarding teacher professional development (PD) routes?

a. Once hired, teachers usually only get PD via professional organizations.
b. Working teachers do not have the time to attend graduate PD courses.
c. Teachers use PD only to get higher degrees/certificates in the same subject.
d. Many teachers learn additional subjects and/or specialties through PD.

98. Among these forms of educator professional development (PD), which kind enables collaborations on presentations and workshops and promotes information sharing?

a. Mentors
b. Study groups
c. Learning communities
d. Pre-service internships

99. Which statement related to teacher professional development (PD) goals and processes is most accurate?

a. US states all certify/license teachers with BA/BS degrees and do not require a master's degree.
b. Teachers earn the same licensure regardless of the PD goals of individual US states.
c. Once a teacher has an advanced graduate degree, there is no need for further goals.
d. PD goals can include reading professional literature as well as taking specific courses.

100. School districts' professional development committees (PDCs) help educators pursue PD by doing which of the following?

a. PDCs work with new teachers and their mentors but never pay workshop tuition.
b. PDCs ensure PD goals meet district guidelines and document PD for state boards.
c. PDCs work apart from district administrators by setting only interdisciplinary goals.
d. PDCs defer to district administrators for setting district professional teacher goals.

Answer Key and Explanations for Test #1

1. B: Pragmatics is the area of linguistic development involving using language socially with other people in order to meet one's needs. One way teachers can help adolescent students develop their pragmatic linguistic skills is to teach them skills for asking questions socially. Teaching them to distinguish between literal and figurative word meanings (a) is a way for teachers to help teenage students develop their linguistic mediation skills rather than their pragmatic skills. While researchers find very high positive correlations between vocabulary and IQ test scores, vocabulary is more likely a function of intelligence than vice versa (c). Therefore, (d) is incorrect.

2. D: Although Attention Deficit Hyperactivity Disorder or ADHD (a) certainly includes inattention, short attention span, and impulsive behavior; students with mental illnesses (b) certainly can have difficulty completing assignments and/or exhibit disruptive class behavior; and assignment noncompliance and acting out in class can certainly be symptoms of behavior problems (c), teachers with more experience and developmental perspectives are more likely than those without these assets to realize such behaviors can actually be signs of adjustment problems. Many students begin middle school in sixth grade. Because schools can vary widely and because of change itself, students can have difficulty making transitions to middle school. The same applies to transitions from middle to high school.

3. B: As Piaget described, adolescents develop the ability to reason abstractly by performing mental operations. They can engage in deductive reasoning, e.g., responding to "if-then" propositions by speculating about possibilities, including hypothetical moral dilemmas as well as their personal futures. Students typically achieve what Piaget called conservation, e.g., understanding that the same amount of liquid exists despite being poured into differently shaped containers (a), by middle childhood. Being able to perform logical mental operations and reverse them (c) is also typical of middle childhood—as long as these concern concrete/physical objects, events, or examples. Symbolic representation (d), e.g., representing things using other objects, images, and words, typically develops earlier in childhood (c. 2-7 years old).

4. C: Although American schools today are legally desegregated, this clearly does not mean the neighborhoods surrounding them also are (A). Hence, community racial and economic limitations strongly influence education. Some Latino parents believe it can overcome discrimination and support bilingual education, but their support does not make it required (B). Some Latino parents believe desegregation impedes their objectives by attenuating Latin influences and destroying bilingual education programs, but this does not mean desegregation is bad overall (D). The most accurate conclusion is that compromise is required, particularly since both school desegregation and appropriate services for English learners are legal mandates (C).

5. A: In *early* adolescence, teens engage in developmental activities including applying their emergent cognitive skills and developing new self-images (b) based on their physiological changes. In *middle* adolescence, developmental tasks include separating from parents, exploring relationships, and experimenting with different ideas and behaviors (c), and developing responsibility, self-reliance, and greater control (d) of their learning and work opportunities and activities, as well as finding their place in society and contributing to it. In *later* adolescence, developmental activities include stabilizing their personal identities and social roles; integrating their worldviews and psychologies and making these more consistent; balancing fantasy, aspiration, and reality; shifting from self-interest to caring for and giving to others; and establishing realistic life goals and pursuing them (a).

6. B: For preadolescents and younger adolescents to resolve Erikson's psychosocial nuclear conflict of Industry vs. Inferiority (typically described as from age 7–12, but individual differences can make it earlier or later), they must experience success in school. For students to transition from Piaget's cognitive Concrete Operations to Formal Operations stage (A), teachers can start them with logical reasoning involving concrete manipulatives and then gradually progress, scaffolding as needed, to abstract reasoning without concrete objects. Forming action plans for the future that they find satisfying (C) is an activity that helps older adolescents to resolve Erikson's psychosocial conflict of Identity vs. Role Confusion. Students typically need to transition cognitively from intuitive thought to logical reasoning (D), i.e., from Piaget's Preoperational to Concrete Operations stage, during early childhood, not adolescence.

7. B: Setting goals for positive social interactions and distinguishing between short-term and long-term goals (a) are appropriate assignments for students in middle school or grades 6-8. Setting short-term goals (e.g., for a hobby, sport, learning a musical instrument, or other activity of interest), planning action steps and time frames for these goals, and evaluating their levels of goal achievement (c) are appropriate assignments for students in grades 8-10. Planning long-term goals, identifying who helped them achieve a goal, and how, and analyzing the impacts of obstacles, unexpected opportunities, scheduling conflicts, and other positive and negative factors on goal achievement (d) are assignments appropriate for students in grades 9-11. Setting long-term goals that include action steps, completion dates, anticipated obstacles, and contingency plans (b) are appropriate assignments for students in grades 10-12. Analyzing present health behavioral impacts on long-term goals, evaluating the feasibility of summer job goals, self-evaluating goal achievement, creating behavioral contracts supporting coping strategies, and journaling goal progress are also good assignments for grades 10-12.

8. A: Adolescents much prefer active, interactive, hands-on, real-world, and authentic learning experiences over passive, teacher-centered lessons that describe subjects without letting students experience them directly and learn by doing. Because of the wide variety of cognitive levels and interests among adolescents, teachers need to provide wide varieties of materials, not narrower ranges (b). As adolescents develop abstract thought, teachers need to provide the more complex, abstract information, concepts, ideas, and sophisticated humor they can now appreciate rather than simpler, more concrete material (c). Teens, particularly young teens, are not as interested in traditional academic content (d) as in real-life and authentic learning. They can learn the same content through more direct hands-on experiences, which make it more real and valuable to them, enabling better retention, generalization, transfer, and application to life.

9. A: Pianta found that training teachers to change their behaviors with students changed the teachers' beliefs more than communicating information to persuade teachers that their beliefs were mistaken. For example, a teacher who believed boys were naturally disruptive quashed a boy's enthusiastic, loud response, resulting in student frustration and emotional disengagement. But a teacher who did not believe boys were inherently disruptive encouraged a loudly enthusiastic boy to continue his response, only while quietly sitting instead. Teacher beliefs dictate their expectations and interpretations of student behaviors. These beliefs were changed more by behavioral training than by information (b); hence these approaches did not have equal results (c) or no results (d).

10. C: Experts recommend that teachers imagine school through their students' eyes to understand them better, contrary to what option A suggests. Experts also recommend that teachers reflect about their own best and worst teachers/supervisors when considering students' perspectives, unlike answer B suggests. Like option C describes, experts recommend that teachers create a list of the feelings they experienced when interacting with teachers and supervisors in their own lives, along with what evoked those feelings. This is meant to gain insight into students' reactions to what teachers say and do. Contrary to what option D suggests, experts recommend that teachers should not focus on their own perceptions of students but rather try to understand how students perceive the teacher.

11. B: As educator expert Robert Marzano has noted, effective instructional strategies include relating success stories to students, which reinforces their efforts in school and helps them see the causal relationship between effort and achievement. Another strategy that promotes this connection is having students keep logs and analyze them (B). Marzano advises teachers to give symbolic, not tangible, rewards to students (C) to recognize their efforts and achievements more effectively, and to personalize or individualize those rewards for each student to make them more meaningful and relevant than uniform rewards (D).

12. D: Research finds that while visual representations both stimulate and increase brain activity (A), students achieve more when taught using both verbal and visual modalities (D). For teaching relationships, both words AND images are effective symbols (B and C). For teaching information, physical models and movements are best (C).

13. B: One recommended way for defining student learning goals and what grades they will receive for meeting those goals is for teachers and students to write and sign contracts agreeing to goal and grade terms. Experts say student learning goals should be compatible with student personal goals, not unrelated (a). They note it is important for teachers to give students specific, timely, and corrective feedback (c). They also recommend that teachers invite students to lead feedback sessions (d).

14. A: Schools can involve students as planners in developing classroom behavior rules, new building designs, and textbook selection, and in planning coursework according to career research. When schools involve students in showing teachers how to use new technology in exchange for learning about all subjects in the curriculum, the role is students as teachers, not professional development partners (b). When schools involve students in collecting and analyzing data and contributing to team development, the role is students as professional development partners, not decision makers (c). When schools involves students in influencing curriculum, school policy, and school climate as members of student government, the role is students as decision makers, not teachers (d).

15. A: When middle and high school students learn to take good notes on class lectures and lessons, reviewing and revising those notes are often the best ways for them to study for tests. Skimming text, storytelling, and using graphic images are ways of varying style in advance organizers (b), which should be analytical and introduced before lessons (c). Having students question, clarify, and make predictions about texts helps them not only understand, but also summarize (d) better.

16. B: When helping students conduct research for writing papers, it will not enable plagiarism to teach them MLA, APA, Turabian, or other official styles (a) of citing and listing references; rather, it will prevent it. So will teaching students the regulations for fair use and copyright laws (b). Teaching students about Creative Commons licensing will not guarantee plagiarism (c) but will help students avoid it when they use Creative Commons sources. Teaching students how to evaluate sources is not the only way of preventing plagiarism (d), but a way of helping students develop critical thinking skills they will use for the rest of their lives.

17. C: Oppositional Defiant Disorder (ODD) affects preschoolers as well as older children. About half of preschoolers outgrow ODD by eight years old; some develop Conduct Disorder (CD) a few years after diagnosis of ODD. CD is more severe than ODD and the most severe psychiatric disorder of childhood. Adolescents who have ODD or CD are more likely (almost 20 percent) to develop Antisocial Personality Disorder, a diagnosis only made in adults, which extends the symptoms of CD. Since these conditions are related and associated with age groups, (d) is incorrect.

18. D: Orientation and mobility (O&M) training is provided by O&M specialists and helps students with visual impairments to navigate school buildings, grounds, and other public environments more independently. In addition to training students to orient themselves and navigate in their surroundings, O&M specialists may teach cane use and work with students and their service dogs. Strobe lights (a) are adaptations to traditional sound-based fire alarms enabling deaf students to perceive alarms. Text-to-speech software (b), magnification, and large print (c) all help visually impaired students read rather than navigate environments.

19. B: Similar classroom behaviors are caused by different disorders. Students with intellectual disabilities (a) may behave inappropriately due to immaturity, lack of understanding, lack of communication skills, self-regulation deficits, and inadvertent adult reinforcement. Students with autism spectrum disorders (c), as well as those with ADHD (d) and communication disorders, may explode from frustration when their needs are not met. ADHD students also often interrupt classes with vocalizations, speech, out-of-seat behavior, and other physical movements, etc. Some behaviors are substitutes for more acceptable communication when skills are lacking.

20. C: Gender affects student learning and performance in that boys are more likely to be aggressive physically, whereas girls are more likely to be aggressive relationally (verbally insulting others, spreading rumors, impugning reputations, etc.). Visual vs. kinesthetic (a) is an example of how different learning styles affect student learning and performance. Cooperation vs. competition (b) is an example of how different cultural backgrounds affect student learning and performance. Inadequate vs. adequate clothes/food (d) is an example of how socioeconomic status affects student learning and performance.

21. A: Locus of control is related to motivation, and particularly achievement motivation. Students with more internal locus of control attribute their successes and failures to causes within themselves, which contributes more to achievement motivation than external locus of control, wherein students attribute successes and failures to causes outside themselves. Self-confidence (b) affects motivation by facilitating attempting new tasks when high or inhibiting this when low. Student maturity (c) affects motivation in that some students have differing levels of physical, cognitive, and/or emotional-social maturity. Cognitive development (d) affects motivation in that students need differentiated instruction if their cognitive levels are higher or lower than those of classmates.

22. D: The ADA (1990) prohibits discrimination based on disability. By giving the same protections based on disabilities as those earlier given based on race, color, national origin, sex, or religion, the ADA was modeled on the Civil Rights Act (a) of 1964. By requiring federally funded schools, facilities, buildings, programs, services, and activities to give people with disabilities equal access, the ADA was also modeled on Section 504 of the Rehabilitation Act (b) of 1973. The ADA was not modeled on the IDEA (c), whose existence under that name* began in 1990 after the ADA; rather, by requiring equal access, opportunity, participation, and benefit from public facilities for persons with disabilities, it predicted the IDEA's extended emphasis and guarantee of inclusion and integration in education for students with disabilities. *(PL 94-142/EHA was an earlier incarnation with a different name: the name change to IDEA marked the extensive revisions accompanying reauthorization.)

23. B: The Individuals with Disabilities Education Act (IDEA) provides a guarantee of the right to a free, appropriate public education (FAPE) in the least restrictive environment (LRE) that can meet their educational needs for students with disabilities. The purposes of the LRE clause are to *prevent* separate/segregated classes/schools for these students (a), and to meet individually differing student needs (b). The IDEA requires IEPs for all students with disabilities, but not for students without disabilities (c). It was enacted initially for school ages (IDEA Part B); another section (IDEA Part C) was added later for early childhood ages (d).

24. C: Section 504 of the Rehabilitation Act of 1973 and the Individuals with Disabilities Education Act both specify a FAPE as a requirement for schools receiving federal funding to provide for students with disabilities. The Americans with Disabilities Act (ADA) (a), (b), (d) prohibits discrimination based on disabilities in access to public buildings, facilities, programs, services, and activities, including public schools. It does not specifically require providing a FAPE.

25. C: Discriminant validity, also called divergent validity, confirms that constructs we expect to be unrelated are in fact unrelated. When constructs are not combined or confused in a test's measurement (a) as they should not be, this indicates the test has construct validity. When constructs we expect to be related are confirmed to be related (b), this indicates convergent validity. When a construct measured by a test given to a sample group can be generalized to a larger population (d), it has external validity.

26. A: When a test (or an experimental research design) shows cause and effect, it has internal validity. External validity (b) is whether or how much a test's results (or research effect) can be generalized to larger populations, other settings, measurement variables, and/or treatment variables. External validity includes ecological validity (c), i.e., how impervious a test or effect is to environmental influences, and population validity (d), i.e., how representative of the population the sample tested is and whether the sampling method used is acceptable.

27. B: Formal assessments are frequently standardized tests, which have been given to large numbers of students, data from their results mathematically calculated and summarized, and standard scores, percentiles, or stanines given. They are best for summative assessment after instruction, not formative assessment (a) during instruction. Their measurements are more generalized, not individualized (c). They are typically norm-referenced, not criterion-referenced (d).

28. D: Informal assessments are often performance-based and/or criterion-referenced tests rather than norm-referenced. They are often not supported by statistics (a) as formal assessments (like standardized tests) are. They are better for providing individualized student data than generalized data (b), which formal assessments better provide. Since they do not compare student scores to the average range of those in a normative sample, they are not used to compare students (c) as formal, norm-referenced, standardized tests are but to measure student performance against established criteria.

29. B: Informal assessments, e.g., rubrics, running records, teacher-made quizzes, performance assessments, etc., are typically used for ongoing or formative assessment to monitor student progress and help teachers improve their instruction based on assessment results. Formal assessments, e.g., standardized, norm-referenced tests, are typically used for assessing overall achievement (A), comparing students to peers, obtaining more objective results (C), and identifying in which percentiles (D) students scored, i.e., what percentage of other students' scores their scores were above (e.g., a student whose score is in the 20th percentile scored higher than 20 percent of the others). Informal assessments may show individual student scores as a percentage or number correct out of the total, one of several possible numbers on a rubric, etc., but typically do not include percentile rankings.

30. B: When teachers use performance continua for assessment, they can describe student performance evaluatively with more precision than when they assign separate grades (A), an advantage. However, for comparing assessment scores among students, classes, or schools, the lack of exact numbers on a continuum is a disadvantage (B). On the other hand, the performance ranges provided by continua are more realistic and accurate than assigning exact numerical scores or referring to cutoff scores (C), an advantage. Except for comparisons (B)—in which case standardized tests are better—the superiority of continua for individualized assessment (D) is an advantage.

31. A: Standardized tests of ability, like IQ, creativity, verbal, numerical, spatial, memory, and other abilities measure student competence, i.e., their capacity rather than what they actually do, which is performance (b). Ability tests do not indicate and do not necessarily predict student school grades (c), which are also what they do rather than what they are capable of doing. Student mental health (d) is measured by some standardized tests, but not by standardized ability tests.

32. D: Standardized achievement tests are summative evaluations usually administered at the end of the school year to assess what students have learned and achieved, not formative evaluations made frequently during ongoing instruction (c). They do not measure convergent or divergent thinking, or domain-specific skills like verbal or quantitative reasoning (a) as standardized ability tests do. They measure what students actually do, not what they are capable of (b) doing, which ability tests measure.

33. C: Standardized achievement test results enable educators to compare an individual student's scores among different school years to assess the student's progress in school. They enable educators to compare individual students to grade peers, but not to students in other grades (a), since standards differ by grade. Since they are typically aligned with state standards, they can assess whether students fulfilled those standards; but being standardized, they do not enable educators to assess fulfillment of learning criteria for individual classrooms (b). They not only allow educators to compare achievement among students in the same class or grade; they also enable them to compare achievement in their school to that in other schools (d).

34. B: Both standardized ability tests (e.g., IQ tests, creativity tests, etc.) and standardized aptitude tests (e.g., preference tests, career tests, interest inventories, and tests of scholastic aptitude like the SAT) measure student potential rather than execution—i.e., what they are capable of rather than what they actually do—not vice versa (a) or both (c). While aptitude tests frequently measure abilities as well as interests, ability tests measure abilities but not interests (d).

35. D: Relative to standards-based education, research shows opportunity to learn is the strongest influence on student achievement at the school level. Therefore, students are given multiple opportunities to demonstrate achievement and repeated practice for skill mastery rather than low grades for poor initial performance (B). At classroom levels, teachers consistently use rubrics or other scoring guides to give students criterion-referenced feedback in frequent formative assessments (D), which are more effective than only norm-referenced percentage scores in annual summative assessments (C). Regular progress reports improve teacher evaluation of learning objectives as well as student achievement more than reporting only annual standardized test results (A).

36. B: The US Department of Education (ED) does fund, but does NOT develop, curriculum standards for public schools. State education departments develop them using federal (ED) funding (c). State standards are available in print and online today; online is the easiest way for teachers to access them, particularly updates to them (c), which can be published online more timely and frequently than printing these. The Common Core State Standards, developed by a consortium of state school officers and governors with ED funding, have been adopted by most US states voluntarily rather than via federal mandate (d).

37. A: Having curriculum standards and associated frameworks gives education stakeholders a common language for communicating the learning expectations they share and discussing educational processes, enabling more effective educational partnerships. Curriculum standards also provide common referents to coordinate, not individualize (b), educational system functioning across schools and districts; clarify common expectations for all students regardless of their individual demographics (c); and provide schools with motivation and focus for organizing, designing, planning, and implementing instruction (d) and assessment.

38. C: In this example of student PE learning, participating voluntarily in athletic activities and becoming accomplished in a specific sport are representative of the affective domain, i.e., developing and applying emotional attitudes toward a subject. Choices (a) and (d) are representative of the cognitive domain, i.e., developing and applying knowledge in a subject. Choice (b) is representative of the psychomotor domain, i.e., developing and applying physical skills in a subject.

39. D: In the most recent revision (Anderson and Krathwohl, 2001), Bloom's Taxonomy follows this sequence: Remember, Understand (a), Apply, Analyze (b), Evaluate, and Create (d). This hierarchy progresses from least to most difficult; hence (c) is incorrect. *(Note: The 2001 revision changed the order, from Synthesis (= Create) and then Evaluation, to Evaluate and then Create, in recognition that the process of synthesizing multiple ideas/sources inherently involves creating new wholes and relationships. It also changed the level names from nouns to verbs.)

40. B: Instructional objectives are influenced by the major behaviorist learning theory principle that only behaviors that other people can observe and measure can be modified. Hence, in applying Bloom's Taxonomy, such objectives avoid vague internal terms like 'Remember' and 'Understand' (choice A) and instead use only action verbs to describe how students must demonstrate learning (choice B). Choice D is incorrect because it suggests measurability is optional, whereas behaviorism emphasizes observable and measurable behavior.

41. B: The ABCD method is an acronym for Audience, Behavior, Conditions, and Degree of mastery to help educators remember the elements to include in an observable, measurable learning objective. Writing at a fifth-grade reading level (A) represents the A element of Audience, which is the fifth-grade students. Rewriting a sentence from past to future tense (C) represents the B element of Behavior. Being given a sentence in past tense (D) represents the C element of Condition. Rewriting a sentence from past to future tense correctly 95 percent of the time (B) represents the D element of Degree of mastery.

42. C: According to experienced teachers, to evaluate technological and other instructional resources, more and better criteria are needed for: evaluating not just individual technology items (A), but the overall function of technology in a given instructional unit; evaluating instructional materials more authentically, not less (B); and evaluating how practicable any unit is to implement (C) considering school and classroom realities. National standards from discipline organizations (e.g., National Council of Teachers of Mathematics, National Council of Teachers of English, etc.), teacher experience, research into subject-specific assessment, AND local school district standards (D) are among the resources educators consult for evaluation criteria.

43. A: Articles documenting research into various learning, theories, practices, results, etc., are professional resources used by teachers to improve instruction. Concrete manipulative objects (b) to assist concept and skill learning, worksheets (c) to enable practice in new skills, and games (d) making needed skill practice more fun and motivational are all examples of learning materials.

44. D: Thematic instruction emphasizes holistic learning across curriculum subjects within real-life, coherent, whole experiences with overarching themes. Cognitive skills are taught in the context of real-world topics, rather than only of academic subjects (a). Its purposes and characteristics also include teaching both broadly enough to enable students to explore subjects creatively (b), and also specifically enough to enable them to apply learned skills in practical use (c).

45. C: Testing a hypothesis requires conducting research, e.g., doing an experiment, making field observations, or administering a survey and analyzing the results. Watching videos (a), reading textbooks (b), and listening to lectures (d)—even while taking notes—are not experiential learning activities because they do not involve hands-on learning activities in which students participate directly. Rather than passively absorbing information, students learn by doing in experiential activities.

46. D: Interactive learning activities emphasize the sharing, exchange, and discussion of ideas, questions, activities, tasks, and learning among students. Indirect instruction (a) overlaps with interactive learning in discussion, for example. Independent study (b) overlaps with interactive learning in certain cooperative learning group exercises. Experiential learning (c) overlaps with interactive learning in role-playing activities.

47. B: Teachers should first review national and state standards, course textbooks, additional materials, and required test preparation materials; create a plan of study; plan instructional units and timelines; make a personal lesson plan calendar; and then write detailed lesson plans within each unit. They should not write lesson plans before making a calendar (A) or planning their timelines (C) for covering each unit, since these will affect the lesson plans. Writing lesson plans before planning units (D) makes no sense, as the lesson plans are components of the units.

48. A: Continuous monitoring and charting not only inform teachers of student progress with individual short-term objectives, enabling them to adjust instruction timely as needed; they also give students visual illustrations of their own learning and immediate teacher feedback, not delayed (b). Teachers can also have students make graphs of their own performance and set goals for themselves (c), enhancing student engagement in learning. However, continuous monitoring is not an activity that gives students practice through independent study (d).

49. C: Scaffolding is temporary support that teachers provide to students to enable them to accomplish tasks they cannot yet achieve alone, and which teachers gradually withdraw as students progress toward task/skill mastery. It ultimately moves the student role in learning from passive to active (a); requires students to increase their current knowledge (b); moves the responsibility for learning from the teacher to the student (c); and moves teachers from playing expert roles to facilitator and mentor roles (d).

50. A: In scaffolded instruction, first the teacher models performance of a new and/or difficult task and asks students to do think-alouds about it. The second step involves collaboration between students and teacher. The third step entails paired or small-group student work on the task, with teacher support as needed. In the fourth step, students practice the task independently.

51. D: One caveat concerning independent instruction is that for students to participate, they must first have developed the skills required for working independently. The ability of students to pursue individual interests in their own styles at their own paces (a); student development of autonomy, initiative, self-confidence, self-esteem (b), etc.; and the benefits to students of how flexibly and adaptably independent instruction can be applied (c) are all advantages of independent instruction rather than caveats.

52. A: Self-contained classroom learning centers supply varied, easily accessed learning materials for self-directed student learning activity. Students can independently study class topics in greater depth in enrichment centers (b), learn specific expertise related to such topics in skill development centers (c), and find out more information, like researching various careers related to these topics, in interest and/or exploratory centers (d).

53. C: Although students work more independently in research projects and other forms of independent instruction than in more teacher-directed activities, teachers still provide students with guidance, but only as needed. Teachers do not assign research questions (A); students develop these independently. Students, not teachers, also locate and access information sources (B) for research. Students write reports or papers to communicate their research results, with teacher guidance (D) if they need it.

54. B: While students love getting out of the classroom, this is not the only benefit of field trips (A): they let students apply knowledge and skills learned in the classroom to real life. Rather than confusing students (C), real-world variations inform them how reality differs from academic conditions. For example, rock samples in school geology labs typically have equal distribution, but in the real world quartz is more abundant; lab samples are often pure, but in the field rocks/minerals are more often mixed. Interaction with nature is a benefit *along with* real, hands-on learning (D).

55. B: Simulations are not done in real life, but are the most realistic of these activities. They enable activities students cannot do in real life, e.g., fighting wars, working in various jobs, marrying, having children, building and managing corporations, etc. Field trips (a) are done in real life. Experiments (c) are typically done in classrooms, labs, or other controlled environments, not real-life conditions. Role-playing (d) is similar to simulations, but less realistic as it does not try to simulate real conditions. Instead, students assume others' roles in speech and behavior, developing empathy, perspective-taking, and social interaction.

56. C: The instructional strategy of having students conduct observations helps them to develop objective thinking, pay attention to important details, and become more perceptive. Today's technology makes simulations much more vivid, interactive, and accessible to students than simulations without technology (A). Games are not only entertaining instructional strategies, but they also offer structure (B) via game rules. Experiments make abstract concepts real to students and enable direct student ownership of learning (D).

57. A: Intrinsic motivation tends to persist longer than external motivation, though it can be more difficult and time-intensive to foster than external motivation. Many students are capable of being intrinsically motivated in school, and intrinsic motivation is often highly effective at motivating a student to achieve success.

58. D: To encourage student development of intrinsic motivation, teachers can connect content to student interests. Intrinsic motivation develops when students find learning personally meaningful, interesting, and relevant to their own lives. Teachers can foster this type of motivation by linking content to students' existing interests, goals, and experiences. Answers A, B, and C are incorrect because they deny the importance of teacher enthusiasm and knowledge of students.

59. B: Research-based strategies found to promote student motivation include not only teacher interest in student learning, but also teacher personal interest (A) in their students' backgrounds and concerns; teacher demonstration of their own motivation and passion as role models for students (B); teacher belief in students' abilities (C) as well as interest in students; and teacher personalization of content for individual students (D).

60. C: Students frequently want to know how they will use academic content in their lives before engaging in it. To meet this need, teachers should give them many different examples (a) and explain what preparation the content will give them for future opportunities. Students also often need to discover underlying principles independently (b), which teachers can enable by providing problems students must reason through, affording opportunities for mastery. Teachers can make cooperative learning effective through positive social pressure (d).

61. B: To help motivate students to learn, teachers can design assignments that offer challenges appropriate to the abilities and experiences of their students rather than giving every student the same challenge (a) regardless of background; set realistic, attainable performance goals and help students to set these (b); use test scores and grades to show student mastery rather than shortcomings (c); and give all students opportunities to attain the highest standards and grades, and avoid grading on a curve (d).

62. A: Experts recommend that for effective communication, teachers make *explicit* transitions between topics by signaling them verbally (B), making mini-summaries of each topic before moving to the next topic (C), and/or establishing the connections between one topic and the next (D). They do NOT recommend leaving transitions between topics implicit for students to infer (A).

63. C: By pausing strategically during their speech, teachers get the attention of students, indicate transitions between topics, and allow time for students to process spoken information. Teachers should vary their vocal speeds and tones to keep students interested in their speech rather than speak monotonously, which hinders comprehension. Vocal projection communicates a teacher's confidence in what he or she is saying and helps students hear speech. Teachers should accord longer wait times for ELL and disabled students to allow longer times for translation and processing of receptive and expressive language.

64. B: While teachers are advised against wearing distracting apparel or making exaggerated gestures (A), appropriate physical movements expressing energy, enthusiasm, and excitement about content and learning are effective (B). Rather than losing student respect, teachers communicate that they value their own utterances when they smile (C). Teachers should stand up straight and maintain eye contact to project confidence; slouching and looking away do not put students at ease (D).

65. D: Chalkboards, dry-erase boards, and overhead projections are useful for showing reasoning visually and teaching dynamically, as well as illustrating processes. Utilizing media need not distract (A); teachers can use media to enhance instructional communication in helping explain, clarify, and illustrate complex ideas. Slide presentations are best for organizing varied content, summarizing ideas, and emphasizing key points (B). Animations and videos are best for imparting a sense of scale and depicting dynamic processes (C).

66. A: Audio, recorded or live, is best for illustrating the sounds associated with various physical processes. Artifacts (c) and other realia (b) are both best for incorporating elements from real life into instruction. Handouts (d) are best for giving detailed visual images and printed/written verbal information to students.

67. C: Based on findings of research into conflict resolution in schools, experts recommend role-playing as an effective strategy because it can introduce humor into the conflict resolution process (A); helps students consider the feelings of others (B); teaches them to view behaviors from others' perspectives and empathize with others (C); and promotes more objective examination of conflicts (D) to gain insights about their origins.

68. D: Among strategies for effective classroom conflict resolution, experts recommend that teachers have students track conflicts they partake of and/or witness over time; record their observations in journals, but keep the identities of participants anonymous; and then discuss various student reactions to these conflicts that they have observed, including the advantages and disadvantages of each.

69. A: Conflict resolution experts advise teachers, based on research results, to instruct students in good listening behaviors, including asking questions as needed but not interrupting others; making eye contact (B) with others while listening to them; avoiding giving others suggestions or advice about what they shared (C); and providing speakers with positive reinforcement by nodding and smiling (D) while listening when appropriate.

70. B: Assigning students to write about conflicts they have been involved in gives them time-out periods wherein they can cool off and reflect about events and their roles in them. Writing does not force students to ruminate over conflicts or extend them further (A); it enables them to analyze what happened, review their feelings, retrospectively consider alternatives (C) they might have chosen instead, and use the conflicts as learning opportunities (D).

71. B: The approach of the teacher's "simple authority statement" authoritatively stops student misbehavior with minimal emotional distress (A); models reasonable, respectful use of authority for students (B); and expresses teacher disapproval of student behavior as objectively as possible (C), and does so immediately (D).

72. A: Experts find it relatively easy affectively to treat students the same way whether they have high or low expectations of them, but more challenging academically because once students are habituated to low teacher expectations, they may feel uncomfortable when teachers offer them greater challenges (although these are ultimately beneficial). Hence equal treatment is not equally difficult in both domains (b), equally easy in both (c), or easier academically (d).

73. B: Teachers can make diversity into a resource instead of a liability by giving students adult responsibilities (a) for collaborating with educators to contribute to planning, coaching, financial and funding activities, etc., which also teaches students varied skills. Explicitly teaching skills for studying, working with teachers, and preparing for and applying to college to students whose parents never attended college helps fills gaps in cultural capital (b) for underrepresented students. Showing personal knowledge and caring about individual students fosters student participation (c). Understanding students' home cultures does help educators understand student behavior in and out of class (d).

74. C: Educators support students in succeeding academically by encouraging parents to participate actively. For example, they can help parents converse in ways that prepare their children for classroom communications. Engaging parents promotes mutual understanding of parent, classroom, and school expectations of teachers and students, supporting student success. Helping immigrant/undereducated parents pursue ESL and GED programs allows parents to better support their children academically. Educators can also involve and help parents by referring them to community resources with arts, sports, and science programs, homework help, etc.

75. B: When educators provide culturally relevant curriculum, students can learn more authentic, interactive language, literacy, and cognitive skills. When teachers make semantic webs about student backgrounds, this can inform lesson planning (a) by validating their experiences, which increases their engagement. Curriculum covering the contributions of diverse student cultures enhances student self-esteem (c). Setting culturally compatible norms and expectations for social learning organization and communication make instruction more effective (d), in both teaching and learning.

76. A: In Dialogic Reading, the teacher reads books with individual students/small groups, incorporating "CROWD" prompts for sentence **C**ompletion; text **R**ecall questions; **O**pen-ended text picture questions; **W**h- picture questions; and **D**istancing text/pictures to student experiences. In Dialogic Reading, the teacher also uses "PEER" prompts, **P**rompting student text discussion; **E**valuating responses; **E**xpanding responses; and **R**epeating prompts on higher levels. Think-Pair-Share lets students rehearse responses with partners who help with corrective feedback and elaboration to prepare for whole-class interaction. Choral response involves unison student responses upon teacher cues after teacher questions, signals, and wait time. Inside/Outside Circle involves students pairing up, conversing, and rotating partners.

77. D: Think-Pair-Share activities involve students' discussing assigned subjects with partners, giving each other constructive feedback, and then applying this feedback in sharing with the whole class. Teachers can use this for both spoken and written student responses. Written Responses, Varying Answers (A) involves students' checking written responses with partners, revising as needed, and reading them when teachers call on them. Written Responses, Same Answers (B) involves students' writing answers to teacher questions on boards and then holding them up upon teacher signaling. Since answer choice D is correct, answer choice C is incorrect.

78. D: In traditional games like Musical Chairs or Duck-Duck-Goose, the majority of children are left out of the fun (b) as competing is emphasized. Hence compared to traditional games, cooperative games not only are organized differently, but also have different effects (a). Cooperative games (Cooperative Musical Chairs/Islands, Cooperative Duck-Duck-Goose, Help, Robots, Cows and Ducks/Frogs and Dogs/Cats and Snakes/Chickens and Goats, etc.) teach children more varied skills, including listening, following directions, movement skills, and problem-solving skills, than traditional games (c). Thus preschoolers both have more fun and learn more skills in cooperative games (d).

79. C: Although kindergartners present as high in energy, they also fatigue quickly and thus cannot sustain ongoing active movement (a). Their short attention spans prohibit extended activities (b). Hence teachers must alternate movement activities with restful activities to prevent both exhaustion and boredom (c) in children. Kindergarteners actually thrive when assigned both independent and small-group cooperative work (d).

80. B: Play develops not only social skills (a), but also academic skills, in all of the main subject domains, including literacy, math (c), science, social studies, arts, and technology (d). For example, play develops print concepts, reading, writing, speaking, and listening in literacy; shapes, number concepts, terminology, prediction, money measurement, and time measurement in math; exploration of the physical properties of materials and of recycling in science; collaboration, developing and following rules, geographic thinking, mapping, and money use in social studies;

drawing and creating things in the arts; and basic computer use and software navigation in technology.

81. B: Because parents often want their home interactions to support their children's learning, some teachers design games and other ideas for home use, which many parents welcome (a). Teachers emphasize how important it is to thank parents for attending conferences (b). Many parents attending conferences ask teachers how they can help their children with school; hence administrators encourage teachers to prepare by having specific suggestions ready (c). After reviewing a few recommended student improvements, teachers advise asking parents to follow up with them (d) in the following weeks.

82. C: Teachers report based on their experience that they can avoid antagonizing parents and students by using tactful phrasing (a) during conferences. Some teachers make a practice of including students in conferences with their parents (b). In fact, some teachers even let students lead conferences about their report cards, portfolios (c), etc. Some teachers also like to agree with students and parents to set one or two goals early (d) and then maintain communication throughout the year about progress toward these goals and future plans.

83. D: Whether or not extracurricular activities are available for students often depends on teacher support. Teachers may serve on committees both during school days and also during extracurricular events and activities (a), e.g., PTA/PTO nights and school Open Houses. Participating in committees enables problem solving for both teachers and students (b). By participating in events and committees, teachers communicate with parents and also show students their interest and support beyond academics (c).

84. A: Teacher participation in committees, projects, and other school functions affords more opportunities for teachers to pursue professional development. School rules and disciplinary procedures are often decided in these functions as well. They also provide leadership for intramural and other athletic events, training in individual content-area subjects, tutoring and contribute to fundraising efforts and crisis management programs. Participation in committees, projects, and school functions is, therefore, not generally a waste of time. Participation in sporting events is not usually required.

85. D: One way teachers can participate in school or district projects, committees, and activities is by contributing to curriculum design and text identification and adoption (D). Teachers can contribute to a great number of discussions and decisions beyond those taking place in faculty, department, staff, and PTA/PTO meetings (A). For example, teachers are well-equipped to serve as members of committees tasked with deciding on special population admissions, reviews, and dismissals (C). Teachers, students, administrators, and others may all benefit from the individual expertise and special interest knowledge teachers contribute (B).

86. C: Experts report that reflective teachers have no fear of either self-evaluation (a) or evaluation by others (b), but rather want their self-improvement efforts to be informed by feedback from other experienced educators (c) and are motivated to improve mainly to serve their students best rather than to receive better appraisals (d).

87. A: Teacher appraisals are most commonly conducted by school administrators, such as the principal. While district officials oversee general teaching quality, they do not usually conduct appraisals themselves. Evaluation by colleagues might occur in some contexts, but this is not the norm. Third-party evaluators are rarely used for routine teacher appraisals.

88. B: Teacher performance appraisal systems evaluate not only whether a teacher's instruction is effective, but also whether it is student-centered (a); whether students participate actively and successfully in their learning (b); whether teachers not only evaluate student progress regularly, but also give students feedback (c) based on these progress evaluations; and not only on the time, materials, and instructional strategies that teachers use, but also their management of student discipline (d).

89. B: Professional communication is one of the areas of teacher performance typically evaluated in performance appraisal systems, as is the teacher's professional development; teacher compliance with policies and procedures, including procedures for operation and other requirements; and improvement in academic performance for all students, not only identified ones.

90. D: Teacher appraisals and evaluations are mostly regulated at state and local levels. While federal regulations did heavily control appraisals in the past, since the passing of the Every Student Succeeds Act, power over teacher appraisals largely rests with the state.

91. B: When students transfer schools, FERPA regulations permit the previous school to provide the new school with student records without consent, since the new school will need the student's records from past schools. FERPA also allows student records disclosure to school officials, but only if they have valid educational interests (a); to appropriate school personnel related to student financial aid (c) for purposes of determining and awarding aid; and to any auditing or evaluating officials, but only those specified (d).

92. D: In general, FERPA requires schools to restrict student records except when a parent or eligible student provides written permission. Only under specific circumstances are schools allowed to furnish student records without prior written consent. Choice D is inaccurate because FERPA does not provide a blanket permission to disclose records to juvenile justice authorities in all states. Instead, FERPA allows disclosure to state and local authorities within a juvenile justice system only when a specific State law authorizes such disclosure.

Below is a full list of the circumstances in which a school does not need to have written consent from a parent or eligible student, as found in the FERPA Law:

- School officials with legitimate educational interest;
- Other schools to which a student is transferring;
- Specified officials for audit or evaluation purposes;
- Appropriate parties in connection with financial aid to a student;
- Organizations conducting certain studies for or on behalf of the school;
- Accrediting organizations;
- To comply with a judicial order or lawfully issued subpoena;
- Appropriate officials in cases of health and safety emergencies; and
- State and local authorities, within a juvenile justice system, pursuant to specific State law.

93. D: By FERPA regulations, schools may disclose student directory information without prior consent (A). This includes names, addresses, birth dates, birthplaces, attendance dates, honors and awards, phone numbers (B), etc. FERPA requires schools to notify parents and eligible students of their FERPA rights annually, but does permit disclosure (C) of this student directory information—provided they give parents/eligible students enough prior notice so they can request non-disclosure (D) if they choose.

94. A: National Education Association is a labor union for educators. The other answer choices are professional organizations but not labor unions.

95. A: The National Association for the Education of Young Children (NAEYC) is a professional organization dedicated to young children, their families, early childhood educators, and early childhood education. Professional organizations include not only the National Science Teachers Association, but also the American Association of Physics Teachers and National Association of Biology Teachers (B); the Council for Exceptional Children, and also the National Association for Gifted Children (C); and the American Council on the Teaching of Foreign Languages as well as the Teachers of English to Speakers of Other Languages (D).

96. B: Educational research studies most often inform teachers about the effectiveness of instructional practices by evaluating them, comparing them, and synthesizing many studies of teaching practices through literature reviews, meta-analyses, and compilations to identify consensus about the most effective ones. Federal education departments (A), state boards of education (C), and local school districts (D) are professional development resources that most often adopt research-based instructional practices for their teachers to apply in their classrooms after research studies have identified these.

97. D: One teacher PD route is professional organizations' courses, workshops, and conferences, though this is not the only way (a). Although teachers must stay at school slightly longer than students, and many stay even later to complete work, school days still end earlier than other workdays; and unlike other professionals, teachers get summers off, so working teachers often take graduate courses (b), both individually and as part of advanced degree programs—not only in their original subjects (c), but often in additional subjects/specialties (d), e.g., adding science to math, ESL to English, special to regular education, etc.

98. C: Learning communities are a type of PD that enables educators not only to share information but also to collaborate on producing presentations, workshops, etc. Mentors help educators develop PD plans; observe and give feedback; share knowledge, expertise, and experience; and give support. Study groups enable information exchange like learning communities but not presentations and workshops. Pre-service internships give educators close on-the-job supervision, practice, and work experience.

99. D: A number of US states issue teacher certification/licensure to bachelor's-degree graduates for one or two years but expect them to gain master's degrees (or other additional certification) in the interim. Teachers earn more advanced licensure when they meet goals established by their US states. Even teachers with advanced graduate degrees must continue setting and meeting goals throughout their careers. In addition to adding credentials, taking courses, and attending workshops, seminars, and conferences, reading professional literature can be a PD goal.

100. B: PDCs work with new teachers and their mentors to ensure teachers' PD goals meet school district guidelines. They do sometimes pay workshop tuition, so answer A is wrong. They also provide documentation for state licensure boards of new teachers' efforts to meet state requirements by approving the teachers' PD plans (PDPs). They collaborate with school district administrators in setting both interdisciplinary and subject-specific, district-wide professional teacher goals, so options C and D are wrong.

Practice Test #2

1. How can teachers inform educational problem solving with knowledge of human development, specifically adolescent cognitive and moral development?

a. Assignments enabling students to view complex ethical or moral issues as black and white.
b. Assignments teaching students to view shades of gray they cannot see in complex issues.
c. Assignments considering moral dilemmas, exploring justice concepts, and solving problems.
d. Assignments addressing discrimination, racism, and sexism that the curriculum should not include.

2. Which of the following educational practices would most address the adolescent characteristic which David Elkind dubbed the "personal fable"?

a. Building student self-esteem while avoiding humiliation, harsh criticism, and sarcasm
b. Self-expression and self-assessment opportunities in reading, role plays, and drama
c. Furthering caring atmospheres, positive adult and peer relationships, group cohesion
d. Explaining to students that changing allegiances are normal and friendship important

3. What is true relative to how student substance use and abuse affects development and learning?

a. Substance use and abuse have not been found to cause, affect, or interact with any mental disorders.
b. The use of alcohol and other drugs interferes with attention, but not motivation to learn and achieve.
c. The damage that using substances causes is temporary and reversible, not permanent or irreversible.
d. The brain and other major organs and systems, not fully developed, can be damaged by substances.

4. Which of the following are impacts that gang involvement can have on adolescent student learning, development, and growth?

a. They protect members from other gangs and adult violence.
b. They meet needs for identity, belonging, rules, and direction.
c. They can end school, jobs, freedom, and life via criminal acts.
d. They have all these impacts on student learning, development, and growth.

5. Among the following statements, which most accurately reflects the roles and relationships of individuality and conformity during adolescence?

a. Although (b) is a concern in some ways, (c) and (d) often become even more important to teenagers.
b. In forming personal identities and defining social roles, asserting autonomy is teens' main concern.
c. Social pressures, teen hypersensitivity to peer perceptions, and social acceptance cause conformity.
d. Conformity to peer norms and group belonging gives teens company for facing adult responsibilities.

6. Among the following strategies that educators can use to facilitate teaching and promote learning, which is an example of counteracting issues related to adolescent peer interactions?

a. Giving students assignments to conduct cooperative learning projects with small peer groups
b. Encouraging students to participate in academic clubs and rewarding them when they do this
c. Supporting student resistance to peer pressure by approving of it when they assert themselves
d. Emphasizing learning experiences requiring group interdependence and positive interactions

7. Which of the following typical challenges for adolescent students is most likely to require referral to counseling as well as other educator interventions?

a. The student practicing gymnastics since childhood who now rebels at coach rigor
b. The student practicing ballet since childhood who develops anorexia and bulimia
c. The student who was a small boy but grows 12 inches in less than one school year
d. The students described in all these are equally likely to require counseling referral

8. Four students all love animals equally, but express it differently and have different individual talents. As an example of helping them make informed educational and career decisions, which one should educators encourage to explore pursuing a career as a veterinarian?

a. The student who excels at gentle handling and beautifying but hates math and science
b. The student who excels at and enjoys all subjects in mathematics and in the sciences
c. The student who excels at rescuing and nursing animals and is average in math/science
d. The student who excels at conservation, protecting species, and captive habitat work

9. Regarding teacher and student roles, which statement is most accurate about instruction and learning?

a. Research studies have demonstrated that to learn, all students need teachers to give explicit instruction.
b. Research studies have found that rote memorization is most effective for learning all types of information.
c. Research studies have found when students participate actively in learning, they become lifelong learners.
d. Research studies find students become more original thinkers when taught information rather than skills.

10. Which of these best reflects the influences of home and community factors on high school teaching and learning?

a. In low-income communities, education is often superseded by economic survival needs.
b. In low-income communities, parents emphasize college more to escape a poverty cycle.
c. In low-income communities, after-school activities and learning centers are more common.
d. In low-income communities, more students want to be the first in the family to go to college.

11. According to experts, which of these are characteristics common to all effective learning groups?

a. All students are actively involved, but teachers are not.
b. Students find group work meaningful and challenging.
c. Teachers assign students to homogeneous groups.
d. Competition is more important than cooperation.

12. When teachers assign students to learning groups, which of the following is a feature that all effective groups share?

a. Students are assessed only as groups by teachers using one instrument.
b. Students need social skills for groups, which are made for social reasons.
c. Students need not understand learning objectives as the teachers must.
d. Students believe they can achieve more learning in the group than alone.

13. Which of the following instructional strategies best represents kinesthetic learning?

a. Providing earphones with audiobooks to accompany printed texts during reading periods
b. Providing movies that include music being studied in class
c. Assigning projects to write a chapter that would fit into a book the class is reading
d. Assigning dance or sports movements as means of learning and demonstrating principles

14. A teacher notices that her students' scores on tests improve after incorporating videos, reading, and hands-on activities into her lessons instead of focusing only on lectures and homework. What is most likely the reason for this improvement?

a. This appeals to the students' various learning styles.
b. The teacher is a poor lecturer, and the other sources of instruction fill in the gaps left by her ineffective lectures.
c. Multiple modalities increase engagement and motivation, thus improving learning.
d. Homework is largely ineffective at supporting learning.

15. Which of the following correctly describes attributes of behaviorist learning theory relative to its use in education?

a. It is not only theoretical but is also equally practical.
b. It applies well to animals but not as well to humans.
c. It allows ambiguity when addressing internal states.
d. It takes a long time, and research has not proven it.

16. In behaviorist learning theory, which technique(s) is/are especially useful for teaching students more acceptable behaviors to replace and meet the same needs as disruptive/otherwise unacceptable behaviors?

a. Shaping
b. Chaining
c. Task analysis
d. DRO and/or DRI

17. Of the following, which most accurately reflects provisions of the 2010 ESEA reauthorization?

a. Rigorous school accountability for student performance; meeting diverse student needs
b. Rigorous school accountability for student performance; meeting disabled learner needs
c. Meeting the educational needs of English Language Learner (ELL) and homeless students
d. Educational needs of migrant worker, Native American, delinquent, and neglected pupils

18. Which of these was one of the provisions of the 2010 reauthorization of the ESEA?

a. Nationwide standards for English Language Proficiency (ELP)
b. Supporting migrant student transitions within each US state
c. Homeless student funds allocated by Title I, not by number
d. Statewide standards for English Language Proficiency (ELP)

19. What statement is accurate regarding characteristics of today's English Language Learner (ELL) student population in the United States?

a. ELL students who speak English fluently have mastered the language.
b. ELL students are now prevalent in all US states, no longer just a few.
c. ELL students are the only ones benefiting by school accommodations.
d. ELL students have higher disability incidence, proven by assessments.

20. According to research evidence-based practices, which of these is included in effective instruction of ELL students?

a. Awareness of prior ELL knowledge, characteristics
b. Placement of ELL students according to ELP levels
c. Avoiding the use of technology with ELL students
d. Selecting texts to keep from overwhelming ELLs

21. Among classroom strategies to meet all students' educational needs and ensure their participation, which of these is recommended?

a. Classroom rules should only be enforced by teachers, never students.
b. Classroom assignments should be meaningful but only in class settings.
c. Classrooms function best when students have a voice in how they run.
d. Classrooms should be organized to keep students from moving around.

22. Which of the following represents a characteristic(s) of effective teachers and teaching, according to research findings?

a. Modeling and demonstrating strategies for tasks
b. Using implicit and indirect instruction techniques
c. Providing ample content in unstructured formats
d. Introducing new material holistically, not in steps

23. In guidelines for creating supportive classroom environments, experts use the acronym "VIABLE." V = students feel Valued. I = students feel Included. A = students feel Accepted. B = students feel a sense of Belonging in cooperative learning groups. L = students feel teachers Listen to them. The E stands for students feeling that teachers do what?

a. Exempt (rules)
b. Encourage
c. Exercise
d. Educate

24. To create positive and supportive classrooms with respect for diversity, which of these is an effective educator practice?

a. Invite parent, teacher, and staff to collaborate for students.
b. Praise finished student products more than effort/progress.
c. Analyze past successes; then focus on them for self-esteem.
d. Avoid providing suggestion boxes as this only invites abuses.

25. Which of these is an advantage of essay questions in testing?

a. Requiring recall rather than recognition
b. Providing students with fewer choices
c. Enabling demonstration vs. description
d. Allowing grading to be more objective

26. Of the following, which is an advantage of multiple-choice tests over essay tests?

a. They take more time to give, answer, and grade.
b. They can cover smaller numbers of larger points.
c. They allow clearer correct and incorrect answers.
d. They do not enable elaboration or greater depth.

27. What is one advantage of portfolio assessments?

a. They are not standardized like many tests.
b. They put more pressure on the student.
c. They show longitudinal student progress.
d. They allow the teacher to spend less time grading.

28. Among the Wechsler tests, which would be most age-appropriate for assessing the intelligence of a normally developing nine-year-old student?

a. WPPSI
b. WAIS
c. WIAT
d. WISC

29. For a student who is nonverbal both receptively and expressively, which of the following tests would NOT be appropriate?

a. PPVT
b. UNIT
c. Leiter
d. Raven's

30. Standardized career assessments and aptitude tests measure all EXCEPT which of the following?

a. Student inclinations for certain jobs
b. Student cognitive functioning levels
c. Student verbal/numerical proclivity
d. Student interest in certain activities

31. Which of these takes place first in the process of producing national or state standardized achievement tests?

a. Publication and public marketing of the tests
b. Administering the tests to student samples
c. Publishing statistical analyses of test scores
d. Proof of the validity and reliability of tests

32. What is true about statistical analyses that authors include when they publish standardized tests?

a. They indicate the degree to which a test is valid and reliable.
b. They show average scores rather than average score ranges.
c. They do not show how many students got the average score.
d. They can generally be used to determine the intelligence of students.

33. Why are many standardized tests called "norm-referenced" tests?

a. Because they follow the "normal" format for standardized tests
b. Because they are the norm for year-end testing in public schools
c. Because they report average scores for student "norm" samples
d. Because they refer to universal norms established for all testing

34. Which of these can educators accomplish by analyzing norm-referenced test results?

a. Compare individual student performance with those in normative samples
b. Compare average but not individual student performance to that in norms
c. Satisfy federal but not state accountability requirements for federal funds
d. Satisfy state but not federal accountability requirements for federal funds

35. Which of these accurately reflects findings about interdisciplinary instruction?

a. Students learn to reason and think better when taught discrete skills.
b. Students are more motivated and engaged through their participation.
c. Students do not learn to transfer skills from cross-curricular instruction.
d. Students find curriculum less relevant when subjects are interrelated.

36. How do teachers find students benefit from interdisciplinary instruction?

a. They gain more complex understandings of every individual discipline.
b. They gain more complex understandings of relationships in disciplines.
c. They gain more complex understandings overall, less in each discipline.
d. They gain more complex understanding in relationships and disciplines.

37. In a sequential model of an effective lesson plan, which of the following steps should come earlier in the sequence than the others?

a. Clarify student understanding and assign students to practice.
b. Teach the main lesson, including active student participation.
c. Connect the lesson with learning standards and expectations.
d. Assign students to write their questions, problems, and ideas.

38. A teacher prepares a lesson plan in eight steps, including an introduction; background information and pre-teaching key vocabulary; brainstorming, questioning, and correcting misconceptions; presenting the main lesson; clarifying understanding; guided practice and review; independent practice; and closure. Which is recommended about how the teacher should allocate time for these steps?

a. The main lesson presentation should be longer than any longest other step.
b. The introduction should be longer than the background and key vocabulary.
c. The clarification and practice/review take longer than independent practice.
d. The time allotted for closure should be longer than any time for practicing.

39. Which statement is accurate regarding the best mobile technology applications available to teachers?

a. They automate but do not customize many administrative tasks.
b. They aid not just attendance and grades but also lessons and rubrics.
c. They require other users all to have the same apps to share data.
d. They are not safe for separate users who can access others' data.

40. Of the following instructional planning partners, which can most collaborate with classroom teachers on integrating student IEP goals into daily instructional activities?

a. A library media specialist
b. A special education teacher
c. A teacher of the gifted/talented
d. Another member of the IEP Team

41. The library media specialist functions in which of the following capacities in collaboration with teachers and other educators?

a. An information specialist
b. A program administrator
c. An instructional partner
d. All these and a teacher

42. How do teachers of the gifted and talented collaborate with classroom teachers most?

a. By working with students and teachers, and as coordinators
b. Only by working directly with gifted or talented students
c. Mainly by giving teachers ideas for enrichment activities
d. More by coordinating special activities with class lessons

43. Which of the following members of a student's IEP team is most likely to administer, score, and interpret student IQ tests?

a. The school social worker
b. The school psychologist
c. The special ed. teacher
d. The classroom teacher

44. Of the following, which is true about paraprofessionals working with classroom teachers?

a. They only give concrete forms of assistance like taking attendance and doing physical work.
b. They assist teachers by scoring tests and grading papers, but are not permitted to instruct.
c. They give differentiated instruction and may observe behavior and collect behavioral data.
d. They are a nice bonus for teachers with oversized classes, but do not provide essential aid.

45. Which of these instructional approaches emphasizes collective responsibility?

a. Inquiry-guided
b. Shared learning
c. Learner-centered
d. Learning community

46. Among instructional strategies that enhance communication and help students develop higher-order cognitive skills, which choice describes one correctly?

a. Establish an atmosphere of urgency in the classroom.
b. Require students to determine teacher expectations.
c. Make idea transitions seamless by not declaring them.
d. Establish organized routines; explain and follow them.

47. Of the following cognitive strategies, which most enables students to evaluate and regulate their own thinking?

a. Metacognition
b. Organization
c. Elaboration
d. Rehearsal

48. To help students develop higher-order thinking skills, which of these should teachers do?

a. Tell students the answers rather than asking probing questions.
b. Have students discover procedural knowledge through teacher demonstrations.
c. Use problem identification and solution only for math and sciences.
d. Have students discover appropriate contexts for applying new skills.

49. Research has found that which of the following applications of computer mediation is most effective in enhancing student attitudes, motivation, and academic achievement?

a. Computer-based instruction (CBI) by itself
b. CBI and CAI combined with regular instruction
c. Computer-assisted instruction (CAI) on its own
d. CBI or CAI, but not both, with regular instruction

50. To be effective, what essential learning element must technology support?

a. Students must have connections with experts in real life.
b. Students must be engaged whether actively or passively.
c. Students must participate in activities via individual work.
d. Students must interact, but do not need to get feedback.

51. Among interactive learning strategies, which of these is most formal and logical?

a. Brainstorming
b. Interviews
c. Discussions
d. Debates

52. Regarding brainstorming as an instructional strategy, which statement is accurate?

a. The quantity is more important than the quality.
b. The quality is more important than the quantity.
c. The accuracy is more valued than the originality.
d. Students have more ideas alone than together.

53. What is a characteristic of cooperative learning groups relative to ELL or LEP students?

a. Their orientations are more amenable to collectivist cultures.
b. They promote collective rather than individual responsibility.
c. They enable asking peers what students do not ask teachers.
d. They are better described by (a) and (c) than they are by (b).

54. Learning activities that involve problem-solving processes apply which levels of Bloom's Taxonomy?

a. Problem solving primarily involves the first three levels of the Taxonomy.
b. Problem solving's multiple steps apply all six levels of Bloom's Taxonomy.
c. Problem solving primarily involves the last three levels of this Taxonomy.
d. Problem solving processes primarily apply only two levels of this Taxonomy.

55. When a student is able to transfer knowledge and/or skills learned in school to different situations, including in real life, which level of Bloom's Taxonomy is involved?

a. The third level
b. The sixth level
c. The fifth level
d. All the levels

56. In Stauffer's (1969) Directed Reading and Thinking Activity (DR-TA), students examine a text title to inform its subject; read the text; determine author purpose; question and clarify the information; give their opinions, connect these to the text; and answer open-ended questions. Which cognitive processes does this activity develop most?

a. Comparison and contrast
b. Prediction and inference
c. Summary and synthesis
d. Analysis and prediction

57. Among the following, which is a research-based teacher practice that stimulates student motivation to learn?

a. Providing criticism that focuses on student errors
b. Criticizing specific performances, not performers
c. Categorizing students into leaders and followers
d. Controlling all learning, evaluation, performance

58. According to a model of intrinsic motivation for academic achievement, what do students do first relative to engaging in learning activities?

a. They first engage in activities that they find interesting.
b. They first evaluate activities on the basis of two criteria.
c. They first disengage in activities not interesting to them.
d. They first engage in activities with extrinsic motivations.

59. Some experts find that students evaluate learning activities by criteria of stimulation and personal control. Which of the following is characteristic of an activity that affords some personal control?

a. It is engaging by appealing to students' curiosity.
b. It affords appeal for students' senses of fantasy.
c. It provides students with some kind of challenge.
d. It is attainable and affords students some choice.

60. Which statement is most accurate about the roles of teacher praise and criticism relative to student motivation and encouragement?

a. Teachers praising student efforts frequently encourage students.
b. Teachers judiciously choosing what to praise encourage students.
c. Teachers praising students too freely inhibit their self-motivation.
d. Teachers who give students any kind of criticism discourage them.

61. Which statement is correct in regard to how including students in instructional decisions affects student motivation for learning?

a. Students perceiving teacher control of instruction tend to develop internal motivations.
b. Students perceiving ownership of content and learning have more external motivation.
c. Students perceiving some control of learning are more likely to be internally motivated.
d. Students perceiving that teachers control all instruction are unaffected by punishments.

62. Multimodal presentations that offer input to multiple senses, and lessons incorporating redundant information, are beneficial to which students?

a. English language learners (ELLs)
b. Students who have disabilities
c. Gifted and talented students
d. These and all other students

63. Which of the following examples of questions that teachers can ask students access the Analysis level of Bloom's Taxonomy?

a. Can you think of synonyms? Other examples? Can you use the word in another context?
b. Does this fit a pattern? What effect does it have? Why do you think the author did this?
c. Which is most effective? What are strengths and weaknesses? What are your opinions?
d. How could you change text features, audience, etc.? Can you create your own version?

64. A teacher asks the class questions about what the main points are in a text, what happened in various text parts, and why certain events or actions transpired. Which level of Bloom's Taxonomy is the teacher addressing?

a. Understanding
b. Remembering
c. Evaluating
d. (a) and (b)

65. If a teacher wants to give students an activity to access the Synthesis level of Bloom's Taxonomy, which of these would be most relevant?

a. Having a class debate about a topic from text read
b. Analyzing author styles and adopting writing styles
c. Producing questions that are based on a text read
d. Drawing concept maps exploring text connections

66. A teacher gives the class an assignment to write criteria reflecting reader expectations for different kinds of texts. Which level of Bloom's Taxonomy does this most involve?

a. Evaluating
b. Analyzing
c. Applying
d. Creating

67. Which of the following is most accurate about teacher redirection of students to other activities as a behavior management approach?

a. Redirection interrupts misbehavior, but it provokes student hostility.
b. Redirection returns behavior to on-task, but it damages self-esteem.
c. Redirection focuses students on target behaviors, but not aversively.
d. Redirection helps, but not as well as confronting the student directly.

68. When students display problem behaviors, which teacher response is most effective?

a. Tell students what they should do the next time.
b. Tell students what they did wrong this time.
c. Assume younger students misbehave intentionally.
d. Assume students with ADHD misbehave purposely.

69. What can teachers accomplish by initially responding to minor student misbehaviors with silence?

a. They can keep themselves from responding inappropriately.
b. They can always extinguish misbehaviors via ignoring these.
c. They can buy time currently without informing actions later.
d. They can think of solutions but not allow students to do so.

70. When students behave unacceptably in classrooms, which specific teacher response most helps students to develop responsibility and self-management?

a. Telling the students how to correct their behaviors
b. Managing behavior when they cannot self-manage
c. Sending the students a message to "Check yourself"
d. Telling students to manage themselves responsibly

71. A "clock focus" strategy is useful with younger students who get restless or go off-task during individual classwork. What does this include?

a. Students remain seated and watch clock minutes as the teacher designates.
b. Students stop work and watch the clock until the teacher's signal to resume.
c. Students stand and watch clock second-hand rotations on the teacher's cue.
d. Students watch as many one-minute second-hand cycles as the teacher says.

72. What accurately reflects a principle of communicating teacher expectations to students?

a. "Do as I say, not as I do" is a principle that applies in this instance.
b. Starting out with achievement contracts is one effective method.
c. Teachers should reinforce expectations periodically for students.
d. Teachers should tell parents their expectations for students only.

73. Which of the following most correctly describes an effective teaching practice for motivating students to meet classroom expectations?

a. Some students are motivated by knowing teachers as real people.
b. Becoming the students' friend will motivate them to work harder.
c. Having students suggest class improvements is counterproductive.
d. Making poor grades final and moving on fosters mastery learning.

74. Regarding teaching, learning, and achievement, what has research found about student-teacher interactions and relationships?

a. Teacher-student relationships influence student behavior but not academic achievement.
b. Teacher-student interaction, communication, and feedback make learning more effective.
c. Students' respect for peers promotes active learning; their respect for teachers inhibits it.
d. The literature omits research into teacher-student relationships relative to achievement.

75. What results do student-student interaction and communication typically include?

a. Most, but not all, students have a voice in small-group discussions.
b. Students are no more likely to share the responsibility for learning.
c. Students benefit from interactions without affecting class direction.
d. Students receive exposure to, and can discuss, diverse viewpoints.

76. What have many research studies found regarding teacher enthusiasm?

a. Teacher enthusiasm is found to have no effect on student learning.
b. Teacher enthusiasm is found to enhance student learning by itself.
c. Teacher enthusiasm with constructive feedback enhances learning.
d. Teacher enthusiasm improves presentation, not positive feedback.

77. Which of these is most accurate about nonverbal teacher behaviors relative to their reflecting teacher enthusiasm and other effects?

a. Effective teachers use their eyes to show excitement, not listen to students.
b. Effective teachers use gestures to communicate enthusiasm, not emotions.
c. Effective teachers use nonverbal behaviors to reinforce verbal expressions.
d. Effective teachers move around the classroom only for monitoring reasons.

78. "Five I's" are components of innovation curriculum (Hiam, 2011): Imagination, Inquiry, Invention, Implementation, and Initiative. Which one is the foundation enabling the others?

a. Inquiry
b. Initiative
c. Invention
d. Imagination

79. Which of the following instructional practices most promotes the innovation curriculum component of Imagination?

a. Writing across the curriculum
b. Most questioning by students
c. Giving students more practice
d. Enabling student self-efficacy

80. Augmentative Alternative Communication (AAC) devices and systems can be low-technology, mid-technology, or high-technology. Which of these assistive communication devices/systems is considered the most high-technology?

a. Dry-erase boards
b. Overhead projectors
c. Text-to-speech software
d. Simple VOCAs

81. How can mentors assist teachers in their instructional activities?

a. They cannot help them address gaps in student content knowledge.
b. They know no more specialized vocabulary than newer teachers do.
c. They can help them decide how to allocate content area emphases.
d. They are unlikely to offer them resources for accessing information.

82. In which of these ways can mentors use their experience to help newer teachers?

a. Mentors can help in planning units, but teachers must address performance standards.
b. Mentors can help in developing higher cognitive skills more than lifelong learning skills.
c. Mentors can help in planning lessons, but only teachers can connect these coherently.
d. Mentors can help in planning for extending and applying text and teacher information.

83. The greater experience and expertise of teacher mentors can support newer teachers in which of the following aspects?

a. Understanding appropriate amounts of material to cover in each lesson
b. Understanding students' greater need for reviews than clear directions
c. Understanding that application of learning supersedes prior knowledge
d. Understanding that task difficulty levels should be randomly alternated

84. What does research show about teacher collaboration in K-12 public schools?

a. Teacher collaboration has no relationship with retaining new teachers.
b. Teacher collaboration correlates positively with student achievement.
c. Teacher collaboration is unrelated to personal satisfaction in teachers.
d. Teacher collaboration is funded and utilized in the majority of schools.

85. Which of the following do experts recommend to foster teacher collaboration?

a. Cultivating senses of individual responsibility in all faculty members
b. Recruiting experienced teachers for induction and mentoring only
c. Recruiting experienced teachers in professional development only
d. School leaders' earmarking resources for supporting collaboration

86. According to case study research, how do teachers most commonly collaborate?

a. Case study research finds that teachers commonly collaborate by doing all these
b. Meeting to review student work and standards, and improve instruction accordingly
c. Forming teams to self-plan professional development and vertically align lessons
d. Regular lead teacher/coach support, data access, and sharing their planning time

87. According to US Secretary of Education Arne Duncan, what will shape public education for future decades?

a. Attracting the greatest quantity, rather than quality, to the teaching profession
b. Retaining the most talented teachers as opposed to attracting more new talent
c. Strengthening the teaching profession with only minimal changes to the culture
d. Requiring massive cultural change yet attaining extraordinary long-term impacts

88. Which of these is most correct about the TEACH.org project for educational reform?

a. It is a public project of the federal government.
b. It is a private project of the Microsoft Corporation.
c. It is a public-private partnership of ED and Microsoft.
d. It is without relationship to the Project RESPECT of ED.

89. What is true about partnerships of schools with families and communities?

a. Schools can use family and community strengths and needs to develop partnerships.
b. Effective family and community partnerships improve learning for certain students.
c. Connections between curriculum and real-world skills are shown via other methods.
d. Partnerships of school, community, and families benefit some, but not all, partners.

90. Regarding school involvement with their communities, which of the following do community needs assessments help school action teams to develop?

a. Approaches for community outreach only
b. Involvement goals leading to full policies
c. Full policies for involvement immediately
d. Involvement program goals, not policies

91. What is true about professional development (PD) goals that teachers set and how PD committees (PDCs) help them with these?

a. PDCs offer training to all teachers, focusing on their school districts' goals.
b. Teacher, mentor, and PDC goals must only meet school district standards.
c. PDCs offer training but do not work directly with individual new teachers.
d. The SMART requirements for writing objectives do not apply for PD goals.

92. Resources like the International Society for Technology in Education (ISTE) help educators do which of these?

a. Develop technology-based professional development programs only.
b. Integrate technology into instruction as well as develop PD programs.
c. Integrate technology into teaching rather than develop PD programs.
d. Teach educators how to use technology but not how to set or teach standards.

93. In-depth professional development (PD) knowledge and standards for educational technology use are taught by the International Society for Technology in Education (ISTE). What would you expect this training to include?

a. Conditions essential for implementing standards at all these levels
b. Conditions essential for implementing standards in the classrooms
c. Conditions essential for implementing standards at the school level
d. Conditions essential for implementing standards for whole districts

94. The International Society for Technology in Education (ISTE), as an example of a resource for integrating technology into teaching and professional development, includes among other offerings Digital Citizenship and Technology Leadership Institutes, a Standards Readiness Workshop, and an Essential Conditions Readiness Survey to which of these personnel?

a. Any and all public school personnel
b. Only teachers and similar educators
c. School principals and administrators
d. Faculty and administrative workers

95. Which statement is most accurate about reflection relative to effective teaching?

a. Hindsight is 20/20, so there is no point in reflecting on one's past practices.
b. When reflecting, teachers as just as subjective as they are in the moment.
c. Reflection enables analyzing and improving interactions but not instruction.
d. Reflection enables improving interactions and instruction based on analysis.

96. How can teachers self-assess their classroom effectiveness using reflection?

a. Wait long enough in the year to establish routines before taking baselines.
b. Make video recordings of all classes to be objective rather than journaling.
c. Select a few students with average class achievement to track relationship.
d. Write honestly in journals and reread entries regularly to change behavior.

97. Among the following reflective methods, which is most suited to helping teachers systematically evaluate their instructional practices, address their teaching weaknesses, and expand their teaching strengths?

a. Peer assessment or "critical friend"
b. Making systematic incident analysis
c. Pre-designed self-assessment tools
d. Collecting and reviewing portfolios

98. According to cognitive research, which of these is better for reading comprehension than for complex concept comprehension?

a. Summarizing
b. Contrasting
c. Comparing
d. Classifying

99. Which higher-order cognitive skills are developed by effective summary and note taking?

a. Analysis, in-depth study, synthesis, and reading comprehension
b. Analysis of learning material but not in-depth, and not synthesis
c. Synthesis of materials but not analysis or reading comprehension
d. Summarizing, contrasting, comparing, and classifying, not analysis

100. Research into educational achievement motivation has found which of these?

a. Students respond better to concrete rewards than they do to abstract recognition.
b. Rewards are most effective when they are not contingent on meeting standards.
c. Eight-year-olds use learning strategies different from those used by 12-year-olds and adults.
d. Negative and positive feedback are both equally effective with eight-year-old students.

Answer Key and Explanations for Test #2

1. C: Adolescents develop the ability to see complex ethical and moral issues not in black and white (A), as younger students do, but in more realistic shades of gray. It is not that they cannot see these (B); rather, adolescents are aware of these nuances but not yet ready to confront them, raising their risk for making faulty ethical or moral decisions. Teachers can use their knowledge of these developmental characteristics to inform their instruction by providing assignments requiring adolescent students to consider moral dilemmas and responses thereto; explore justice, equity, and fairness concepts; solve problems (C); and develop their own values and set their own behavioral standards. While teachers' assignments should address discrimination, racism, sexism, and similar issues, school curriculum should also do so (D).

2. B: What Elkind named the "personal fable" is the adolescent delusion that one's problems are completely unique and nobody else has experienced and can understand or relate to them. Providing opportunities for self-expression and self-assessment through reading, role-play, and drama can help teenage students realize that their problems are not unique but are in fact common, even universal. Building student self-esteem and avoiding humiliating, harshly criticizing, or sarcastically speaking to/about them (a) would address the adolescent characteristics of low and fragile self-esteem, exaggerated self-consciousness, and hypersensitivity to criticism. Promoting caring atmospheres, positive adult and peer relationships, and group cohesion (c), and explaining to students that changing allegiances are normal and friendship is important (d), would both help to support adolescent identity formation.

3. D: In adolescence, the brain, nervous system, heart, lungs, liver, kidneys, and other major organs and systems are still not fully developed yet, and they are thus more vulnerable to damage from using alcohol, drugs, and other substances. For example, myelination, i.e., the development of coating sheaths that facilitate neural transmission and protect brain and nerve cells, which normally continues into adulthood, can be disrupted by substance abuse. Research confirms that using substances can precipitate or exacerbate mental disorders (A) including anxiety, depression, paranoia, bipolar disorder, schizophrenia, and others. Using alcohol and other drugs interferes not only with attention, but also with memory and motivation to learn and achieve (B). Using substances can cause temporary, reversible, permanent, and irreversible damage (C).

4. D: Although most adults know gangs encourage or peer-pressure adolescent members into criminal acts that can end their educations, jobs, freedom, and ultimately lives (C), not everyone realizes gangs also confer certain benefits, e.g., protecting teens against violence from other gangs and adult criminals (A), and meeting needs for behavioral direction, personal identity, group belonging, and rules (B). Adversarial relationships are more secure than complex, equivocal, uncomfortable realities; concrete foes are more beatable than larger, more abstract foes like crime, no opportunities, discrimination, illiteracy, and poverty. Hence, gang involvement both negatively and positively affects adolescent development and learning.

5. A: Although in terms of separating from parents, forming their personal identities, and defining their social roles, asserting their autonomy is important to adolescents (b), it is typically not their only or most important concern. Hypersensitivity to peers' perceptions and concern with social acceptance are hallmarks of adolescence, motivating teens to conform to group norms (c). Conforming and belonging to groups not only relieves their hypersensitivity to criticism and exaggerated self-consciousness, but also helps teens feel they are not alone in facing coming adult responsibilities (d), which they may feel threatened by in defining their individuality.

6. C: By asking students what is right for them, not for everybody else, and showing their approval and pride when students assert themselves, educators facilitate teaching and promote learning by supporting teenage students in resisting peer pressure through counteracting peer interaction-related issues. Other ways that educators address these issues can involve exploiting them rather than counteracting them, including assigning cooperative learning projects with small peer groups (a), encouraging and rewarding participation in academic clubs (b), and emphasizing other learning experiences requiring group interdependence and positive interactions (d) that promote both collective and individual learning.

7. B: Eating disorders are serious, and can be fatal if untreated. However, many patients recover with therapy. Educators can also offer choices, encourage conversation, communicate that perfection is impossible and unnecessary, and offer things the student can control other than her body. The student who complied with strict coaches during childhood but now rebels while developing individual identity (A) may respond to educator help deciding whether to quit or continue, perhaps with less competitive roles, shorter hours, or different coaches. The student whose precipitous growth spurt changed his height and appearance (C) can benefit from educator input that his changed appearance, leg pain, and tendency to become winded from running and climbing are normal, thus offering some assistance in adjusting his self-image. Since choices A and C are incorrect, choice D is also incorrect.

8. B: Educators can encourage the student who both loves animals and excels in mathematics and sciences to consider a career as a veterinarian, a medical doctor requiring more education and training than physicians treating humans; the student who hates these subjects but excels at gentle handling and beautification (a) to consider a professional pet groomer career; the average math and science student who excels at rescuing and nursing animals (c) to consider working as a veterinary technician or in an animal rescue organization; the student concerned with wildlife conservation, protecting endangered species, and working to improve captive animal habitats (d) to consider becoming a wildlife biologist or zoo curator. Students may share a common interest, but need educator help relating it to different individual higher education and career decisions.

9. C: Research studies find that students become lifelong learners when teachers allow and require them to participate actively in learning. Some students do need explicit instruction, but not all do (a). Research finds that rote memorization is effective for learning only factual information, not all types (b). Teaching learning and thinking skills to students produces more original thinkers than only teaching them information (d).

10. A: Regardless of student and parental interest in education, just surviving economically often supersedes it. Parents in high-income communities more often have attended college and thus expect their children in high school to attend college as well (B). Educational resources and supports like after-school activities, learning centers, tutoring centers, and stores selling educational products are more common in high-income than low-income communities (C). Although some students in less educated families and low-income neighborhoods are motivated to be the first in their families to attend college, those who do are in the minority rather than the majority (D).

11. B: In all effective learning groups, teachers give group assignments that students find meaningful and that challenge them. Teachers are always actively involved (a) in group learning processes as coaches, guides, questioners, evaluators, and resources. Teachers assign students to heterogeneous groups (c). Cooperation is always more important than competition (d) in cooperative learning groups and their work.

12. D: One feature shared by all effective learning groups is that students believe they can achieve more by learning in the group with classmates than they could by learning on their own. In all effective learning groups, teachers are able to assess students both individually and as groups, and by using multiple, varied assessment instruments (a). Students do need social skills for interacting in groups; however, groups are not made primarily for social reasons (b). Just as teachers must understand group learning objectives, they must also ensure that students also clearly understand them (c).

13. D: Kinesthetic learning is that which involves physical activity and hands-on experience. Dance or sports movements as a means of learning or demonstrating principles are examples of kinesthetic learning. Choice A is an example of auditory learning. Choice B is an example of a visual and auditory learning. Choice C is an example of linguistic/verbal learning.

14. C: Multiple instruction modalities (e.g., videos, reading, listening, and hands-on activities) can improve engagement and motivation in the instruction material, which can improve outcomes. Incorporating multiple modalities can also require students to integrate knowledge in new ways and engage learners to work harder to understand the material. Learning styles are no longer generally recognized, so option A is not correct. While it is possible that the teacher is a poor lecturer, the real benefit of introducing the other methods of instruction is that they improve engagement and motivation regardless of the teacher's skill as a lecturer. This makes option B not the best answer. Option D is incorrect because homework is generally considered an effective way of supporting learning.

15. A: Behaviorism is not only a learning theory but also a very practical (a) tool for changing behaviors when applied to real-life situations and students. It applies equally well to humans as to other animals (b); unlike some other psychological theories (e.g., psychoanalytic or cognitive), it works regardless of intellectual level. Behaviorism restricts all analysis and modification to observable, measurable behaviors, so it eliminates much ambiguity by NOT addressing internal states (c). It can change behaviors much faster than other methods, and much research has proven its techniques and characteristics (d).

16. D: Differential Reinforcement of an Other Behavior (DRO) and/or Differential Reinforcement of an Incompatible Behavior (DRI) are behavior modification techniques that are especially useful for teaching more acceptable replacement behaviors. DRO trains a behavior the student likes/accepts by reinforcing (rewarding) it; DRI trains a behavior, also by reinforcing it, that the student cannot engage in concurrently with the unacceptable behavior. Shaping (a) by reinforcing successive approximations toward a target behavior, and chaining (b) by connecting individual behaviors, are especially useful for teaching students to adjust to transitions between activities. Task analysis (c) by breaking tasks down into smaller, more manageable steps is especially useful for teaching complex tasks to students with intellectual or cognitive disabilities.

17. A: The 2010 reauthorization of the Elementary and Secondary Education Act (ESEA, aka No Child Left Behind) provides for rigorous school accountability for student performance and also for meeting the needs of diverse students. These include students with disabilities (b); ELL students; homeless students (c); migrant workers' children; Native American students; delinquent students; and neglected students (d). Only (a) summarizes all these; all the other choices omit a number of these provisions.

18. D: One of the provisions of the ESEA's 2010 reauthorization was for each state to implement statewide, *not* nationwide (a), standards by grade level for ELP. Another provision was to support the *interstate,* not within-state (b), transitions of migrant students into local schools and communities. An additional provision was to allocate funds for homeless students by number of students, *not* by Title I shares (c) as was previously provided.

19. B: Whereas ELL students were prevalent in only a few US states in the past, today they are in every state. Teachers should not assume speaking fluent English indicates mastery of the language (a): basic English spoken in everyday social interactions differs markedly from academic English; proficiency can only be assessed through systematic academic assessments. Accommodations implemented by schools for ELL students benefit not only those students, but also native English-speaking students (c). ELL students do NOT have more disabilities (d): research has proven that assessment instruments failing to separate ELL status from disability lead to misdiagnosing ELLs as disabled.

20. A: Knowing what prior knowledge and experiences ELL students have, as well as their individual learning characteristics (e.g., strengths, weaknesses, styles, preferences, etc., in their native languages) enable teachers to make their instruction the most effective. Placement of ELL students should be according to their academic achievement, not their ELP (English Language Proficiency) levels (B). Teachers should not avoid using technology (C), which helps ELLs be motivated to learn, develop English-language writing and editing skills, communicate in English print as well as speech, and collaborate on class blogs and websites. Another practice found effective in instructing ELLs is to give them choices of texts (D), not to have the teachers select the text for them.

21. C: Classrooms are found to function best when students have a voice in how they run rather than having school districts, administrators, and teachers dictate this. Teachers should also assign students to enforce classroom rules (A). Teachers should give assignments that are not only meaningful to students but are also completed in real-life settings rather than only in class (B). They should also organize their classrooms to enable students to move around (D), access information and technology easily, and visit centers or stations for long-term learning activities.

22. A: Research findings show that modeling (especially for special education students) and demonstrating (for all students) the most effective strategies for approaching and completing school tasks are included among characteristics of effective teachers and teaching. Also included are using explicit and direct instruction techniques (B), structuring all content provided (C), and introducing new material step by step, not as a whole (D).

23. B: The "VIABLE" acronym represents that students will develop both self-respect and respect for teachers and other authority figures when they feel Valued, Included, Accepted, a sense of Belonging, Listened to by teachers, and Encouraged by them—not exempted from rules (a), exercised (c), or educated (d) by them.

24. A: Inviting and involving parents, other teachers, and school staff to collaborate in meeting student needs by solving education and discipline problems is an effective practice for creating positive, supportive classrooms with respect for diversity. Answer B suggest praising finished products more than effort, but effective practice is to praise student effort and progress rather than only finished products. Answer C is incorrect because teachers should analyze students' past successes with them to learn from them, but then focus on the present. Answer D is incorrect because it gives students a "voice and choice" rather than only inviting abuses.

25. A: Essay questions require students to recall, i.e., retrieve information from memory without seeing it, rather than simply recognize correct and incorrect information provided as in multiple-choice tests. Essay questions afford students more choices, not fewer (b), as they can choose subtopics, points to make, examples to give, differential emphasis, various organizational methods, the option to use argumentation, etc., whereas multiple-choice questions only offer choices of several answers. Essay questions require description, not demonstration (c); performance measures enable demonstration, which benefits students who cannot write as well as they can do things. Grading essay questions is more subjective (d) than grading multiple-choice or other objective questions.

26. C: Multiple-choice questions have clearer correct and incorrect answers, whereas essay questions allow every individual student to answer differently, requiring more judgment of teachers in grading them. Multiple-choice tests take much less time to administer, answer, and score (A)—and may even be scored electronically instead of by teachers—than essay tests. They can cover larger numbers of smaller points, not vice versa (B), compared to essays. The fact that they do not enable students to elaborate or go into greater depth (D) to show more of their knowledge is a disadvantage, not an advantage, of multiple-choice tests.

27. C: Portfolios accumulate student products over longer time periods like semesters or school years, showing the student's longitudinal progress better than a single test or paper. The fact that portfolio assessments are not standardized like many formal tests is not an advantage but a disadvantage, as the results are less objective and uniform. Portfolios put less pressure on students by letting them work more gradually than on more time-limited tests. Portfolio assessments still have to be graded like any other assessments. In fact, the lack of standardization could lead to longer grading times in some circumstances.

28. D: The Wechsler Intelligence Scales for Children (WISC) is for assessing IQ in students aged from 6 years to 16 years 11 months. The Wechsler Preschool and Primary Scales of Intelligence or WPPSI (a) is for assessing IQ in children aged from 2 years 6 months to 7 years 7 months. The Wechsler Adult Intelligence Scales or WAIS (b) is for examinees aged 16 years to 90 years 11 months. Wechsler Individual Achievement Test or WIAT (c) is not for assessing intelligence; it is an achievement test.

29. A: The Universal Nonverbal Intelligence Test or UNIT (B), Leiter (C) International Performance Scale, and Raven's (D) Progressive Matrices are all intelligence tests designed to be completely nonverbal. The Peabody Picture Vocabulary Test or PPVT (A) does not require students to speak, write, or sign; they can simply point to pictures (physically disabled students can use directional eye gaze or adaptive equipment), so it does not require expressive language; however, it does require receptive language to understand the examiner's verbal prompts. Hence it would not be appropriate for a student who is both receptively and expressively nonverbal.

30. B: Standardized aptitude tests measure student inclinations for specific job areas; for example, they may identify student ability and interest in teaching, mechanical work, or writing; composing, producing, and/or performing music; dancing and/or choreography; drawing, painting, and/or sculpture; mathematical computation; writing computer code, etc. Some aptitude tests measure student ability and interest for types of activities (D) rather than specific jobs/job areas, e.g., working outdoors, working with books, building things, fixing things, communicating with others, etc. Some test student proclivity for broader domains, like verbal or numerical thinking and activities (C). Aptitude tests can measure all these, EXCEPT student levels of cognitive functioning (B), which IQ/ability tests measure.

31. B: After designing a standardized test like a national or state achievement test, the authors must first administer it to groups of students they have selected as representative samples of the larger target population. The next step is conducting and publishing statistical analyses of the student samples' test scores (C). Statistical analysis helps provide evidence of the test's validity and reliability (D) and the numerical degree of each. Following these, the authors can publish and market their test (A).

32. A: Statistical analyses of standardized tests indicate whether the test has been found statistically valid (i.e., whether it tests the construct it is supposed to test), reliable (i.e., whether the test can be replicated with consistent results across administrations, raters, and/or within itself), and to what degree numerically. They may identify the average score received in student sample groups or the average score range depending on the authors and test. They often indicate the percentage of students receiving the average score or score range. They also often include how all other scores are distributed in addition to the average score/range. Standardized tests cannot generally be used to determine the intelligence of students.

33. C: Standardized tests that are called "norm-referenced" are tests that have first been administered to samples of students found representative of a test's intended student population, with their average scores determined (as well as the distribution of all other scores beyond the average score/range) so educators administering them thereafter can compare their students' scores to these averages, which are used as norms—i.e., typical scores for students in that population. The term "norm-referenced" does not refer to a "normal" format (A), to the common practice of giving these tests in public schools as summative assessments (B), nor to any kind of universal norms for all testing (D).

34. A: By analyzing the results of administering norm-referenced tests to their students, educators can compare the performance of individual students with that of students in the normative samples. They *can* also compare their students' average score to the average scores in the norm samples (b). They can satisfy *both* federal (c) *and* state (d) legal accountability requirements for federal funding by showing sufficient scores, because the federal education department delegates many decisions about allocating federal funds to state education departments.

35. B: Educational research finds that when students participate in learning across the curriculum, they are better able to realize the value of the knowledge they acquire, making them more motivated and engaged. Students also learn to reason and think better when taught skills integrated across the curriculum than when taught isolated skills (a). By experiencing the interrelationship of subjects, students learn *better* to transfer skills they learn to other contexts (c). Curricula become *more* relevant to students, not less (d), when they learn how the subjects are interrelated.

36. D: Teachers find students gain more complex understandings not only of each individual discipline (a) and of the relationships between and among disciplines (b), but of both (d). For example, students might study botany in the classroom, learning information from texts; conduct hands-on plant-growing experiments, making and recording observations and measurements; participate in a field trip to a forest; draw diagrams and illustrations of plants; and write reports. Their teachers have thus integrated academic and experiential learning with reading, science, math, art, and writing. Therefore, (c) is incorrect.

37. C: In one sequential model of an effective lesson plan (Cunningham, ASCD, 2009), the eight steps are: (1) Introduction, (2) Foundation, (3) Brain Activation, (4) Body of New Information, (5) Clarification, (6) Practice and Review, (7) Independent Practice, and (8) Closure. Clarifying understanding and assigning practice (A) is part of step 5. Teaching the main lesson, including active student participation (B), is part of step 4. Connecting the lesson with learning standards and expectations (C) of what students will learn is part of step 2. Having students write their questions, problems, and ideas (D) is part of step 8.

38. A: According to the author (Cunningham, 2009) of a model for an eight-step lesson plan, the introduction should take 5 minutes, while discussing background and pre-teaching key vocabulary should take 5–10 minutes (B). The main lesson presentation should take 10–15 minutes (A). Clarification should take 5–10 minutes, and guided practice and review should also take 5–10 minutes, but teachers should allot 10 minutes for independent practice (C). Closure should take 5 minutes (D).

39. B: Today's mobile applications not only automate but also customize many administrative tasks (A) for teachers. They not only make taking attendance and recording grades much easier and faster but also enable teachers to plan lessons and create rubrics (B) more simply and quickly. They enable other users to share and access data across different devices and applications (C) via flexible user interfaces and integrated Dropbox and other storage programs. Today, good applications commonly include protection features to guard data safety for separate users (D).

40. B: The special education teacher has the most expertise of those listed for collaborating with classroom teachers on integrating student IEP goals into daily instructional activities. Library media specialists (a) can best collaborate with teachers and help students in locating, accessing, and evaluating information and other resources. Teachers of the gifted/talented (c) contribute special expertise with this population; however, many students with IEPs have other exceptionalities, with which special education teachers are more familiar than they or other IEP team members (d).

41. D: Library media specialists function as information specialists (a) by finding and evaluating information and showing students and educators how to do so; as program administrators (b) by administering library media programs and directing their activities; as instructional partners (c) by connecting information with curricula, student needs, and school expectations of students, developing policy, practices, and curricula and collaborating with teachers; and as teachers (d) by working with students directly.

42. A: Teachers of the gifted and talented not only work directly with these students (b) by instructing them, but also give classroom teachers ideas for enrichment activities (c) to provide for the gifted and talented students in their classes; they also help classroom teachers to coordinate these special activities with the teachers' regular classroom lessons (d) and/or units.

43. B: The school psychologist is most likely to administer, score, and interpret student IQ tests, as well as other psychological and behavioral testing: collecting and analyzing data, and providing behavior management plans and training, counseling, consultations, referrals, etc. The school social worker (a) coordinates special services, helps families locate and access resources, and provides student and family histories, etc., but typically is not trained in psychological testing. Special education teachers (c) and classroom teachers (d) are also typically not qualified to administer, score, and interpret IQ tests.

44. C: Teachers' aides and other paraprofessionals not only give concrete assistance like taking attendance, activity setup, materials distribution, helping with adaptive devices and other physical work (a); they also score tests and grade papers for teachers (b); with training, give one-on-one differentiated instruction and supervision impossible for one teacher to give every student; and with training from school psychologists, may observe student behaviors and collect data (c) for teachers. Hence they are not simply a bonus, but provide essential (d), even vital, services meeting excessive demands on teachers and helping students achieve individual educational goals.

45. B: The shared learning approach to instruction emphasizes the collective responsibility for learning of students, teachers, other educators, school staff, school administrators, parents, community members, and other stakeholders. The inquiry-guided (a) approach emphasizes student responsibility for independently investigating and learning. The learner-centered (c) approach requires students to take responsibility for learning and teachers to take responsibility for facilitating it. In the learning community (d) approach, each member of the learning community takes responsibility for participating and realizing learning goals.

46. D: When teachers establish organized routines and instructional activity sequences, explain these to students, and follow them consistently, this promotes both teacher-student communication and student cooperation, productive work, and higher-order thinking skills. When teachers establish comfortable, non-threatening classroom atmospheres, this is more effective than a sense of urgency (A). Clearly communicating clear teacher expectations is more effective than making students guess them (B). Teachers should inform students of transitions between ideas rather than not identifying them (C).

47. A: Metacognition involves thinking about and understanding one's own thought processes, which enables self-evaluation and self-regulation of one's own thinking. Organization is a cognitive strategy of arranging material with a structure that makes order and sense of it. Elaboration is a cognitive strategy of producing additional explanation, details, etc., about a topic. Rehearsal is a cognitive strategy of practicing information for retention.

48. B: To help students discover procedural knowledge, teachers can explain procedures and demonstrate how to apply them. Asking probing questions rather than telling students the answers, not vice versa (A), improves comprehension, decision making, problem solving, and application of concepts, principles, and procedures. Teachers can also help students develop higher-order thinking skills by giving them practice in identifying and solving problems in art, music, and writing as well as math and sciences (C). Teachers should explain which contexts are appropriate or inappropriate for applying new skills, not expect students to discover them (D).

49. B: Research has found that combining both CBI and CAI with regular classroom instruction enhances student attitudes, motivation, and academic achievement, rather than only using CBI (a), only using CAI (c), or combining only one or the other but not both with regular classroom instruction methods (d).

50. A: Integrating technology into instruction must support curriculum goals. Four essential elements of learning that technology must support are connections with real-life experts (A); active student engagement, not passive; group participation by students; and not only frequent student interaction but also frequent feedback to students.

51. D: Brainstorming (a) is more characterized by informality than formality, and more by creativity and originality than logic. Interviews (b) may be formal (structured), informal (unstructured), or a combination of both (semi-structured). Though structured interview questions have a logical sequence, interviews including affective topics may not be logical. Classroom discussions (c), while including rules (e.g., taking turns, avoiding cross-talk, disagreeing civilly, etc.), tend to be more informal, allowing students to express themselves.

52. A: Regarding brainstorming, the quantity is more important than the quality. The idea is for students to generate as many different ideas as possible, regardless of how viable, popular, etc. Thus (b) is incorrect. When students brainstorm, it is more important for them to produce original ideas than to be accurate (c). An especial strength of brainstorming as an interactive instructional strategy is that students get more ideas together than they could alone (d).

53. D: Cooperative learning groups are oriented to interdependence and value cooperation above competition, making them more compatible with many ELL/ELP students' collectivist cultures (a). The principles of cooperative learning promote *both* collective and individual responsibility (b) and accountability. When ELL/ELP students are culturally inhibited from asking certain questions of teachers, cooperative learning can make them comfortable asking these of classmates in their groups (c).

54. B: Problem solving includes multiple steps that involve knowing information, understanding it and understanding relationships, analysis, divergent thinking, and evaluating solutions and their results, effectiveness, and value. Bloom's levels in order are: Remembering, Understanding, Applying, Analyzing, Evaluating, and Creating; problem solving involves all of these, not only the first three (A), last three (C), or only two (D).

55. A: When a student can transfer knowledge or skills learned in school to different situations, including in real life, this reflects Applying, the third level of Bloom's Taxonomy. The sixth level (b) is Creating (formerly called Synthesis), i.e., generating new ideas through combining learned information rather than applying it. The fifth level (c) is Evaluating, i.e., assessing and judging information and using it as a basis for estimating or predicting rather than applying it. The first level is Remembering (retaining and retrieving information), the second Understanding, and the fourth Analyzing (breaking information down into components). Since (a) is correct, (d) is incorrect.

56. D: The DR-TA develops analysis by having students analyze text to determine its author's purpose, question and clarify its information, connect their opinions with it, and answer questions about it; it develops prediction by having students predict text subject matter by examining its title. It does not directly develop comparison and contrast (a), which involves identifying similarities and differences within/among texts; or inference (b), which involves extrapolating unstated meanings from text; or summary (c), which entails distilling and concisely restating main text ideas; or synthesis (c), which requires combining information in new ways.

57. B: Among research-based practices whereby teachers can stimulate student motivation to learn, one is to criticize a specific performance by a student rather than criticize the student. Teacher criticism should also be constructive, i.e., focusing on what students can do better or differently rather than focusing on student errors (A). Teachers should avoid categorizing students as leaders or followers (C). They should also give students as much choice and control as possible over their learning, evaluation, and performance rather than teachers' controlling all these completely (D).

58. A: According to a model of intrinsic student motivation to achieve in school, students first engage in activities they find interesting. If an activity is not immediately interesting to students, they then evaluate these based on two criteria (B): stimulation and control. If an activity subsequently becomes inadequate to either or both criteria, they then disengage from it (C) unless they are influenced by some extrinsic motivation (D).

59. D: A characteristic of personal student control in a learning activity is some free choice—e.g., in specific topics, methods, procedures, learning styles, materials, and assessment formats for learning and demonstrating learning. Personal control over a task also includes it not being too difficult for a student to accomplish. Task appeal to student curiosity (a), sense of fantasy (b), and task challenge (c) are all characteristics of stimulation, i.e., how stimulating a task is to a student.

60. A: Research has found that frequent teacher praise encourages students (A) to want to learn. Teacher praise should be frequent and offered freely to encourage students, and being too judicious with praise should be avoided, as praise should be given for all student effort (B). This type of freely offered praise promotes rather than inhibits self-motivation (C). While negatively oriented criticism might discourage students, constructive criticism from teachers does not (D); it encourages them and promotes self-motivation.

61. C: Students are found more likely to develop internal motivation for learning and achieving in school when they perceive that they have some control over their own learning. Students who perceive that the teacher controls instruction are more likely to develop external than internal motivations (A); students who perceive ownership of their own learning and the content they learn are more likely to develop internal than external motivation (B). When they perceive that teachers control all instruction, students are more motivated by external rewards and punishments (D) than internal factors.

62. D: All students with all characteristics—those learning English as a new language (a), those with various disabilities (b), the gifted, talented (c), and creative, and all other students, including the "average" and those without exceptionalities—receive benefits from multimodal presentations and redundant information. In general, people tend to learn more material more effectively when instruction incorporates redundancy.

63. B: Questions about whether text or other material fits any pattern, its effect(s), and why the student thinks the author used certain material, devices, or techniques access the Analysis level of Bloom's Taxonomy. Questions about synonyms, examples, and contextual word use (a) access the Application level of Bloom's Taxonomy. Questions about the material's effectiveness, strengths, and weaknesses, and student opinions of it (c), access the Evaluation level of Bloom's Taxonomy. Questions about changing text features or audiences, etc., and students' creating their own versions (d), access the Synthesis or Creation level of Bloom's Taxonomy.

64. D: By asking students what happened in text, the teacher addresses Remembering (b), the first level of Bloom's Taxonomy; by asking them why things happened and what the main points are in the text, the teacher addresses Understanding (a), the second level in Bloom's Taxonomy. These questions do not address the fifth, Evaluating (c) level, which would involve asking students what they think of the material, how effective it is, its assets and liabilities, etc.

65. B: The class activity of analyzing author styles and adopting certain writing styles is most relevant to accessing the Synthesis level of Bloom's Taxonomy, as students compare styles and use them to create something new. Debating a text topic (a), writing text-based questions (c), and drawing concept maps to explore connections in text (d) are all more relevant to the Analysis level of Bloom's Taxonomy, as students examine material and break down its components.

66. A: Writing criteria that reflect reader expectations for various types of texts most reflects the Evaluating level of Bloom's Taxonomy. An activity to reflect the Analyzing (b) level could be debating a topic from a text(s), making concept maps of connections in text, writing questions about text, etc. An activity to reflect the Applying (c) level could involve writing examples from other sources of a textual concept or feature. An activity reflecting the Creating (d) level could include studying and writing text in various genres, etc.

67. C: Redirecting students from disruptive, inappropriate, or off-task behavior to classroom activities interrupts the misbehavior without provoking student hostility (a). Redirection returns them to on-task behavior without damaging their self-esteem (b) by calmly reminding them of assigned tasks rather than criticizing their behaviors. It helps students focus on target behaviors without communicating aversive feelings or judgments (c). Redirection is a useful alternative when it is unnecessary or unwise to confront a student directly (d).

68. A: The most effective teacher response for behavior management when students display problem behaviors is to tell them what they should do instead next time. This corrects their behavior, but prevents discouraging them by focusing on the future instead of telling them what they did wrong this time (B). Teachers should not assume that younger students (C) or those with ADHD (D) always misbehave on purpose when a lack of impulse control is often the reason. In such cases, teachers can curtail misbehavior by calmly redirecting students to learning tasks without impugning their motives.

69. A: When student misbehaviors are not significantly disruptive, teachers can keep themselves from responding inappropriately (A) as they might in reacting immediately by initially responding with silence. They cannot always extinguish misbehaviors by ignoring them (B): extinction only works when the behavior's sole function is to get attention and attention is withheld; the student eventually stops the behavior for lack of reinforcement. Silence can buy time currently, enable teachers to make mental notes to inform which actions may apply later (C), and allow students time to solve their own problems (D).

70. C: Giving students a "Check yourself" message implicitly communicates that by checking, they will realize what they must do to correct their behaviors. It is more effective for developing responsibility and self-management to remind students to check themselves and let them realize what to do than telling them what to do (A), managing their behavior for them (B), or simply telling them to manage themselves responsibly (D) without giving them any specific means of doing so as telling them to "Check yourself" does.

71. C: In the "clock focus" strategy, the teacher prearranges a cue with students. When they get restless or go off-task, the teacher gives the cue and students stand and watch the second hand on the clock rotate to complete a full minute. Students decide how many rotations to watch and then sit down and resume working. They do not remain seated, and the teacher does not designate how many minutes to watch (A and D). The teacher does not signal them when to resume work (B).

72. B: One effective method for communicating teacher expectations to students is preparing achievement contracts defining mutual teacher-student expectations and having students sign these when school years begin. Teachers lead by example in modeling integrity for students by always behaving fairly and consistently in class, showing how they meet their own high expectations so students understand better what is expected of them; "Do as I say, not as I do" does NOT apply (a). Teachers must reinforce expectations daily for students, not periodically (c), and repeat them continually. Teachers should tell parents their expectations for both students and parents (d).

73. A: It is true that some students are motivated to work harder to please teachers when teachers get to know them and let students see them as real people. However, this does not mean teachers should become students' friends (b): they must stay in charge. It is not counterproductive, but enhances student knowledge, engagement, and ownership of expectations, to have students periodically write about how they think they are progressing and offer suggestions for improving class (c). To foster mastery learning, teachers should let students revise any work that received poor grades (d).

74. B: Research finds that when teachers learn about their students, interact and communicate with them, and give them appropriate feedback, the relationships they develop make teaching and learning more effective. The research has accumulated a significant body of literature showing the influence of teacher-student relationships on student academic achievement as well as behavior (a); hence (d) is incorrect. Teacher respect for students and guidance of students to respect each other promotes active learning; student respect for teachers does not inhibit it (c).

75. D: When students are given opportunities to interact and communicate with each other, they can hear and consider each other's ideas, and every student can have a voice, particularly in small-group discussions (a). Student-student communication promotes student sharing of the responsibility for learning (b). Another benefit of student-student interactions is that students can shape the direction of the class (c), as well as being exposed to and discussing diverse viewpoints (d).

76. C: Many research studies have found that when teacher enthusiasm is combined with constructive feedback, students are able to learn with enhanced quantity and quality; hence (a) and (b) are incorrect. Research studies also find that teachers who are more enthusiastic devote more time both to their instructional presentation and to positive feedback (d) about student performance.

77. C: Effective teachers use nonverbal behaviors not only to express excitement, but also to reinforce verbal expressions (c) of encouragement, etc. They express excitement by opening their eyes widely, raising eyebrows, etc.; express interest and connection with eye contact; and listen to students (a) with their eyes as well as their ears. Gestures like hand movements, body swinging, and sweeping arm motions communicate enthusiasm, pleasure, displeasure, amusement, disappointment, disapproval, and other emotions (b). Effective teachers move around the classroom not only to monitor students, but also to maintain student interest by being less predictable (d).

78. B: Initiative is the foundation that enables the other four components of innovation curriculum by initiating them and supporting individualized, decentralized learning activities. Inquiry (a) involves student curiosity, questioning, exploration, and research toward innovation. Invention (c) involves applying learning to real life and improving problem-solving skills on a regular, not occasional, basis. Imagination (d) involves generating divergent alternatives and creative expression.

79. A: Writing across the curriculum is an instructional practice that stimulates student Imagination by combining arts, sciences, and other subjects and extending universal instructional themes across content areas. Having students instead of teachers ask most of the questions (B) promotes student Inquiry. Giving students more practice (C) applying what they learn promotes student Implementation. Developing student self-efficacy (D) through teachers' challenges, encouragement, and support promotes student Invention.

80. C: Text-to-speech software, like speech-to-text software, other software programs, adaptive hardware, and computers themselves, are considered high-tech AAC devices/systems. These devices and systems are more complex and expensive. Dry-erase boards, like folders, binders, albums, and other easy-to-use, inexpensive image transmission and storage mechanisms, are considered low-tech. Overhead projectors are considered mid-tech. Simple Voice Output Communication Aids (VOCAs) are considered mid-tech.

81. C: Based on their greater teaching experience and expertise, mentors can help teachers by giving them ideas and strategies to address student content knowledge gaps (a); informing them about specialized subject vocabulary (b); helping them with decisions related to relative emphases on various content areas (c); and offering them resources for accessing information (d).

82. D: Mentors can help teachers plan instructional units so they align with performance standards (a); offer teachers strategies for developing higher cognitive skills and skills for lifelong learning (b); help teachers with writing lesson plans and also with connecting lessons coherently (c) within units; and help teachers plan varied challenges, activities, and other experiences that require and enable students to extend and apply information they have acquired from their texts and teachers (d).

83. A: Mentors can help newer teachers to understand appropriate amounts of material to include in each lesson; equal student needs for clear directions and regular reviews (b); the importance of activating and building upon prior student knowledge, including connecting it with new learning, as well as of applying new learning (c); and understanding that task difficulty levels should be increased gradually and sequentially (d).

84. B: Research shows that teacher collaboration correlates positively with student achievement, so Choice B is correct. Choice A is incorrect because collaboration is associated with higher new-teacher retention, not the absence of a relationship. Choice C is incorrect because collaboration is associated with greater teacher satisfaction, not being unrelated. Choice D is incorrect because collaboration and mentoring are still used in only a minority of schools, even in states that provide funding for such programs.

85. D: Experts recommend that to foster collaboration among teachers, school leaders should earmark resources for supporting classroom observation, planning, and mentoring. Choice A is incorrect because effective collaboration depends on shared responsibility among faculty rather than an emphasis on individual responsibility alone. Choices B and C are incorrect because collaboration is not limited to using experienced teachers in only specific contexts; instead, experts recommend schoolwide collaboration that includes induction, mentoring, and professional development.

86. A: Case studies by researchers find that teachers collaborate by meeting to review student work, see if it addresses state/district standards, and improve instruction accordingly (b); forming teams to self-plan their own professional development and to align lessons across grade levels (c); receiving regular support from lead teachers or coaches; and accessing data to inform instructional decisions and planning, as well as sharing their planning time (d).

87. D: Secretary Duncan has said in multiple speeches that the near future of public education will be shaped by attracting the most talented individuals to the teaching profession rather than the largest numbers (a), and also retaining the most talented teachers (b), which he believes will require not just minimal (c) but "massive" cultural changes, but will be worth it by attaining "extraordinary" long-term impacts (d).

88. C: The TEACH.org project to improve future teacher preparation and hence student education was started by the US Department of Education or ED (a) and then reformed as a public-private partnership with the Microsoft Corporation (b). Another ED initiative, Project RESPECT (Recognizing Educational Success, Professional Excellence and Collaborative Teaching), is related to the TEACH.org project (d) and recruits teacher input about teaching reform, federal budget proposals, education in the global economy, etc.

89. A: By gathering information through meetings, interviews, and surveys, schools can identify family and community strengths and needs as bases for developing policies and programs to involve and partner with them. Broad-based community involvement and effective partnerships are found to improve learning for all students (b) by showing them connections between school curriculum and real-world skills (c). School, family, and community partnerships are found to benefit all partners (d).

90. B: By conducting community needs assessments, school action teams can develop not only approaches for community outreach (A) but also goals for involvement programs that they can further develop into full policies (B) for community involvement. They would not develop full-blown school policies for community involvement immediately (C) but develop involvement programs with goals first. They should not stop at these goals but continue developing them into full involvement policies (D).

91. A: PDCs offer trainings that every teacher can take, which help them align their PD goals with those of their school districts. Goals that teachers, their mentors, and the PDCs set must meet the standards of their state education departments (B). In addition to offering trainings, PDCs also work directly with individual new teachers (C) and their mentors to help them set PD goals that meet district guidelines. The same SMART requirements for writing objectives also apply to PD goals (D)—Specificity, Measurability, Attainability, Relevance/Results-orientation, and Time-limitation.

92. B: The ISTE helps educators both develop technology-based professional development (PD) programs and also integrate technology into instruction (B) rather than only the latter (C). The ISTE also has established standards for educational technology application, and instructs educators not only about these standards but also about how to use peer coaching and classrooms to teach them to others (D).

93. A: ISTE teaches in-depth PD knowledge and its own educational technology standards to educators. This includes instruction in what conditions are essential for implementing these standards in classrooms (b), throughout schools at the building level (c), and across entire school districts (d). For comprehensive educational technology integration, one would expect such training to include the classroom, school, and district levels.

94. C: The trainings named are designed for and offered to school principals and administrators, not to all public school personnel (a), not to teachers and similar educators (b), and not to both faculty and administrative workers (d). These trainings target the roles, responsibilities, backgrounds, and perspectives of administrators relative to technology integration in teaching, learning, and educator professional development.

95. D: Although there is truth to the saying, "Hindsight is 20/20," this does not mean reflecting is pointless (a): it reinforces the fact that while we view our behaviors subjectively or not at all in the moment, reviewing them later affords more objectivity (b). Teachers who reflect regularly on their classroom work can identify behaviors and areas needing improvement, and plan and implement improvements accordingly—to both their interactions with students and their instructional practices (c)—based on their analysis of these (d).

96. D: To use reflection for self-assessing classroom effectiveness and planning and implementing improvement measures accordingly, teachers should record baseline levels as early in the school year as possible rather than wait (A). They can make video recordings for objective documentation when feasible, but regular journaling (B) is more practicable and indispensable for developing reflective skills. To show, often accurately, the learning opportunities they offer all students, teachers should select one high-achieving and one low-achieving student and track how their professional relationships with each develop (C). Writing honestly and rereading their entries regularly help teachers change their own behaviors (D).

97. C: Peer assessment and the "critical friend" method (a), wherein colleagues give teachers observational feedback on their instruction, help teachers by noticing things the teacher does that s/he cannot see and offering different perspectives. Systematic incident analysis (b) helps teachers gain insights into student behaviors and their interactions with students. Collecting and reviewing portfolios (d) helps teachers review their longitudinal work development and changes. Pre-designed self-assessment checklists, questionnaires, and other tools (c) are best for helping teachers systematically evaluate their own instructional practices, weaknesses, and strengths.

98. A: Research finds that summarizing content from texts, discussions, lectures, notes, etc., helps to improve student reading comprehension while contrasting (b), i.e., identifying differences; comparing (c), i.e., identifying similarities; and classifying (d), i.e., grouping things by similarity and organizing groups by difference or level. All of these help to improve student comprehension of complex concepts.

99. A: Cognitive research studies have determined that learning to summarize material and take notes effectively develops students' higher-order cognitive skills for analyzing material, examining it in depth, synthesizing multiple sources, and reading comprehension. Summarizing, contrasting, comparing, and classifying (d) information develop student comprehension of complex concepts more than they develop student analysis, in-depth study, synthesis, or reading comprehension of information.

100. C: Research into educational achievement motivation has found that students actually respond better to abstract recognition than to concrete rewards (a); rewards are most effective when they are contingent on meeting some specified performance standard (b); eight-year-olds use learning strategies that differ radically from those used by both 12-year-olds and adults (c); and positive feedback is overwhelmingly more effective with eight-year-olds than negative feedback (d).